Inside Left

Inside Left
Published by The Conrad Press Ltd. in the United
Kingdom 2023

Tel: +44(0)1227 472 874

www.theconradpress.com
info@theconradpress.com

ISBN 978-1-916966-06-2

Cover image: TV interview in the author's front garden
during the height of the COVID-19 pandemic

Typesetting and cover design by
Michelle Emerson michelleemerson.co.uk

The Conrad Press logo was designed by Maria Priestley

Printed and bound in Great Britain by Clays Ltd,
Elcograf S.p.A.

Inside Left

ROGER TRUELOVE

CONTENTS

PART 1
1944-1974

1

HEALTH COMPLICATIONS

On 30 December 2015 I had an outpatient's appointment at Medway Hospital. In forty-nine years this has been my local acute hospital and it has always had a reputational problem, exacerbated by under resourcing. So, they try to be very helpful, to improve patient perceptions.

Just before my appointment at three-thirty they posted an apologetic notice saying they would be running about forty-five minutes late because of a 'patient with complicated issues.'

I do not like being in hospitals but phlegmatically I got out a book to read, only to be called immediately into a consulting room.

My wife, Christine, followed me in and we soon realised who was the patient with the 'complicated issues.' A nervous locum for my consultant said we would have to wait for the McMillan nurse. She soon arrived and together they said I had prostate cancer and that it was serious. After a period of questioning, Christine and I adjourned with the nurse who carefully mapped out the options for treatment which in the end amounted to radiotherapy. She really was exceptionally kind and helpful.

We drove home. I sat and watched some cricket from South Africa. We ate and we then went to our local pub for a drink and a chat. We talked around all scenarios including the possibility that it might be terminal.

At first, I coped quite well but over the next few weeks I experienced some mood swings, increased by taking bicalutamide pills that reduce testosterone levels. At times there was a nauseous feeling in my stomach but at others I upheld a staunch determination to face down something that so many others must face.

At first, I could not help noticing how ever present the word 'cancer' is in our daily lives. Famous people die of it, as David Bowie and Alan Rickman did then. Letters keep coming through the door for cancer research. There are often sad stories in local papers but I felt a little stalked when I walked into a building society and was confronted by a pamphlet asking us all whether we have 'ever been worried by cancer'?

I had to tell family and friends and wanted to do it in a way that minimised the drama. One of my sons was visibly shocked and said it was unfair. One friend said prostate cancer was not that serious and others congratulated me for taking it stoically.

That was helpful.

The lowest point of the day at first was the early morning, waking and reminding myself that I had something that I really would prefer not to have. I felt something similar during the Covid 19 lockdown.

We would have breakfast and, as we have done for years, did the Guardian Quick Crossword together. Working out that funny business (7-6) is jiggery pokery is a very small boost to your self-esteem but it is not a gilt-edged guarantee of anxiety relief.

Work helped. At the time, I was a Councillor on both the Swale Borough Council and the Kent County Council. There were plenty of diverting matters to concentrate on; dealing with people's problems over housing, parking, planning, school places and the inevitable English pothole. There were still plenty of meetings to attend and a period of robust debate would leave me much more energised and a lot less introspective.

The first significant hurdle was to find out whether the cancer had spread to my bones. It had not and that was a real relief. I then had to wait four months to be enlisted on a programme of radio therapy at the Maidstone Oncology centre. My GP Paul Staker was a mountain of re-assurance, honest and realistic but very supportive. A previous GP in the practice asked me pointedly whether I knew what high morbidity meant. He got an expletive affirmative answer.

By April my mood had radically changed and I began to believe all would be well. A group of us men convened at Maidstone, were shown a film of chaps still playing golf during their treatment. The use of golf in these circumstances seems quite common. It is not quite clear what the clinical impact might be if you do not like golf.

Us chaps had to be prepared for radiotherapy, to start in May.

Part of that preparation involves the fastening of a metal stud on to your prostate, an invasive process too delicate to describe in graphic detail to the general reader. Given the location of the prostate there are various other implications surrounding your bladder and bowels that need to be considered.

I got a fairly immediate reminder that this can be a source of prurient humour.

On the day that I had been fitted up for treatment, I went to a charity comedy evening. Someone in our local Labour party was lucky enough to know Josie Long and she came along and was entertaining. But she had also brought along some distinctly tyro comedians.

The first one started with some puns based on the names of fish. It may have been that our local party members were peculiarly unresponsive to fish jokes. Or, the jokes may not have been funny. I am inclined to think the latter.

Struggling for a bit of empathy he thought he would try some jokes about men with prostate cancer. The focus for intended hilarity was pretty much around the procedure I had experienced in the day and I suspect those who had experienced something like this were not amused, whilst the rest did not know what he was on about. It is amazing and quite heroic for individuals with no charisma and little aptitude for humour to subject themselves to the humiliation of nobody laughing with them. As with the fish puns, he tanked.

The treatment which started in May 2016 lasted thirty-seven days. Christine and I made our daily trip to Maidstone, taking up nearly three hours for a maximum of five minutes therapy. I was told to drink enough water

6

to move the bladder away from the area of treatment. This was forty-five minutes before radiotherapy. The summer of 2016 culminated in our referendum on leaving or staying in the European Union and I was consumed with interest in this. Every day for forty-five minutes I read a book by Gordon Brown on the economic consequences of leaving the single market and so the time passed comfortably.

At least it was comfortable in a physical sense, though I was concerned that Brown's warnings would not be heard. I was concerned too that the prime minister and the leader of the opposition seemed considerably less well versed than Gordon Brown.

The care and consideration provided by the hospital staff was outstanding and I felt I had friends by the time I left. The friends came from all round the world, including Europe, Africa, and the Indian sub-continent. In the end I was emboldened to ask why there were so few British radiographers and it was, I was told, because we had neglected to train people for so long in order to concentrate on chemotherapy.

As time went on the water drinking began to present some problems, as the need to relieve my bladder began to reach a peak too soon before treatment. I hung on gamely but by the end I was having to rush out of the treatment room in some desperation. I remember one day I was in real difficulty when one of the radiographers came out and said I had to wait another fifteen minutes. This was critical. I outlined the state I was in and he suggested 'letting some of it out.'

I said 'I don't think it really works like that.' I just had to manage, which I gamely did but my exit from the treatment room was even swifter than usual.

Other men suffered distressing side effects during the treatment, which I did not. It ended in July and in August I saw my consultant.

That wait for a post treatment assessment is one of the most melodramatic parts of the whole experience. I was nervous but exceedingly eager for news. I had made quite a journey from anxiety to positivity in the last eight months and sort of believed that the news would be good.

Detection of prostate cancer is a little hit and miss and relies on a blood test called PSA. Mine should have been about four but over a period of about two years it had advanced to over twelve and so prior to my appointment in December I had had an intrusive biopsy that had led to the diagnosis. I had met other men whose PSA had gone up to 150.

Therefore, I was very relieved when Mr Taylor told me mine was now nought point three and that henceforth I would simply need a blood test every six months to check on my PSA.

It is nearly eight years later now and my PSA is still very low. It can change and I know that and I do regard these intervening years as a bonus.

I feel very lucky and it has had an interesting impact on me over the last eight years. Having had a passing engagement with potential morbidity, I take other challenges much more easily on board.

Well, what has this got to do with this memoir?

In the early stages of my diagnosis, I started writing these recollections. I enjoyed it enormously and it turned days that could have been morose into a kind of uplifting creativity. However, as the threat diminished the writing did too, and to be frank, my attempts to complete the picture have been intermittent over the last few years.

These have been quite stimulating but diverting times.

It is only now in October 2023 that I feel it is appropriate to finally complete the narrative.

And here we are in 2023 and I have much to be thankful for. My personal life is a happy one. I am lucky to have the family and friends I have, and I still get a great deal of reward from my interest in politics.

However, I do have negative feelings.

It is the state we are in. As a country and as a human race, we face a cocktail of dangerous problems, in a political climate that appears to me least able to deal with those challenges. In our own country we have descended into a state that has created an understandable loss of trust. At this moment we are governed by a minority within a minority, with an ever-declining grasp of the existential issues we face and apparently pledged to preserve the interests of a few. Much of the public feel powerless, and when they are given a say, they must make their judgements through a prism of false and distorted messages.

Now, I have divided these recollections into three ages.

First is the period from birth to the age of thirty. I was brought up in a family of high expectations, both

9

academically and in sport. I was obsessed by the game of cricket and to a lesser extent football. For much of my early years, my two brothers were very important to me. I graduated from a modest grammar school in London to do history at Oxford University and then started a teaching career that included working in East Africa. By 1974 I was married with two children and we moved to teach at the Isle of Sheppey in Kent.

Over the next twenty-three years, I pursued a trident of ambitions that somehow collided with each other. I made progress in my teaching career and was Deputy Head of a good secondary school from 1983-1995. But I did not become a Head Teacher.

Secondly, I spent an inordinate amount of time in youth cricket administration, at all kinds of levels from school to international level. Then in 1992 I swiftly withdrew from this activity, at least at a national level.

Because, gradually, from 1981 onwards I had become more and more focussed on my interest in politics, not in a way that I would possibly over dignify as a career, but it steadily preoccupied my consciousness, to the detriment of my other interests.

Consequently, during the last quarter of a century, my political activity has been the principal focus of my daily life, apart of course from my family. My transition from being a Liberal Democrat parliamentary candidate to serving the Labour Party in a myriad of ways obviously represents a watershed for me.

It has realistically been a heavy focus of my wife's life too, something she never bargained for when she married a young teacher with a yearning to go to Africa, and apparently no interest in politics.

I hope friends and family will want to read this memoir because it pretty much says all I have to say. Family, education, sport, and politics are the recurring themes. These may be too eclectic a mixture and I might have succeeded more by being more selective. But I could not do that. I would have found that too restrictive.

I have called these memories Inside Left. I think that pretty well sums up my ideological outlook but it also recalls a now redundant football position from a time when I was so absorbed by both football and cricket. I played every position on the football field except goalkeeper, but my preference was always for *Inside Left,* though at times I found myself on the left wing.

2

ROOTS

I was born on 8 December 1944. My mum and dad had three sons. Owen was seven years older than me and Jim four. Just before the second world war they bought a semi-detached house at 97 Bastion Road, Abbey Wood, on the south east fringe of London. It cost them a few hundred pounds. It would now cost over £450,000.

The road was L shaped and we lived on the corner of the L and because the longer stroke of the L was at a higher level, we had front, back and top gardens, the top garden at one time being used to keep chickens.

At the back was a field where we played football and cricket and beyond that we could walk into Bostall Woods, which stretched a couple of miles down to Lesness Abbey, founded in 1178 by Richard de Lucy, Chief Justiciar of England, as a penance for the murder of Thomas Becket. It was closed during the dissolution of Monasteries by Henry VIII. In the middle of the woods was a bandstand and open space, the focus of much community entertainment in the summer evenings. Elsewhere in the woods, there was a large clearing area that was the venue for scouting activity. It was possible to walk to our primary school, entirely through the woods. There was a very steep slope that was ideal for tobogganing in the winter. Whilst I was part of what Tony Hancock called Baden Powell's lot and required to attend church at St. Nick's, my mum used to meet me and we would walk down to the abbey.

It was a good environment to grow up in. We had the alternative of walking in a more westerly direction towards Plumstead, over Winn's and Plumstead Commons, where local football and cricket pitches were provided. For many years, the common still had prefabricated houses from the Second World War and we had friends living there. Those friends had lived next to us in Bastion Road. Just as our mum had coped through the war with two very young boys and a husband permanently away, the situation next door was similar but not comparable. They had three daughters but the father was absent throughout the war, not braving the high seas and the prospect of German attack, but retreating away from London for fear of bombing. It is no surprise, of course, that women often showed more courage and fortitude than their male partners

Most people locally were comfortably well off for the time, moving from post war rationing to growth in the 1950s, with women able to bring in second incomes with the help of labour-saving household items. It was also a solidly Labour area.

The immediate post war generation instinctively supported public intervention in the lives of people, saw the need for a growing welfare state, and sought after greater equality and less privilege. Most of our respectable road displayed Labour Party posters at election time. Families were also highly aspirational and respected traditional values. Clement Attlee was their natural tribune in the early post war years. I wonder whether Labour can take Bastion Road for granted in 2023. Perhaps we can.

My dad was a merchant seaman. He was a boatswain on ships run by the Blue Star Company. He had come through the second world war, a fearful time for merchant shipping. He continued to go to sea until the mid-1960s.

My mum worked full time for most of my childhood. She ran a shop for a laundry, her own family originally owning a laundry business in west London. She worked to provide a good life for three boys; it was tough and exhausting for her and she experienced bouts of profound frustration. She received regular payments from our dad but I think he retained more than he should have done. Sometimes mum would be struggling whilst he was enjoying such overseas glories as the Melbourne Cup, a horse race by the way.

My dad had been brought up in Gravesend in Kent. His father had been a Trinity House pilot, a position of some social status in the Thames area. Dad was privately educated and throughout his life retained a distinguished veneer. On leave, he would get dressed like a gent and work the paddock at any available horse race course.

He never talked about his early life, but there was a time of year when he could be very morose and tearful. It was the anniversary of his mother's suicide. I believe he was rather disorientated as a young man and never used his full potential, because he was an able man.

For many years I only saw him intermittently. We were always pleased to see him home and he would then try to assert some authority. It is hard to imagine what he thought it was like when he was not there. His favoured focus of domestic interest was food. Given restraints on time and money, my mum fed us well, but when dad came home, we moved into more exotic options, especially expensive joints of meat. There was a small price to pay because we were not really enfranchised to eat without paying due homage to the perfection of the meat. 'Lovely bit a beef that' he would say and we all dutifully chorused our assent. Mum was something of the chorus mistress on these occasions.

After a couple of weeks leave, it was plain that he was keen to get back to sea, to his work. It was perhaps a comfort zone, just like some people only feel at home in military service, in a social milieu of certainty, regimentation and prescribed relationships.

When I was at university, I took a holiday job as a merchant seaman, on a seven-week journey to South America. I hated the physical and recreational restrictions involved but I could understand how men feel safe there, particularly those who do not find relationships easy. When home, dad spent a lot of time at our local working men's clubs, but I am not sure he really fitted in. There was a tendency to ingratiate himself, not least through dispensing some generous largesse. After some trips to Australia, we were introduced to kangaroo's tails which we were persuaded made excellent soup. There had also to be allocations for acquaintances down the club, who were ostensibly very grateful. I asked one of them to tell me frankly what he thought of kangaroo's tail soup. 'Disgusting' was the vivid response. On my one trip to sea, I discovered how much respect there was for my dad and affection for his thoughtful leadership skills. It was enlightening.

When I was five, I came home after isolation in a local hospital. Throughout the 1950s there was great concern around the risk of children catching polio. In this country it was known as infantile paralysis and I was suspected of having contracted it. I spent about a month in an iron lung before it was decided that the symptoms had passed and I could go home. I walked through the door, saw my brother on the stairs and just said hullo Jim. My dad burst into uncontrollable tears. He had thought I was going to die.

My mum's father had died at the end of the First World War in 1918, serving on the front even though he was past the legal age of conscription. His name was Owen Underdown and to my mum and my aunt he was everything that could be good about a man, not least, they said, because of his great sense of humour. I knew I was being flattered if they said to me 'you are not unlike your grandfather.' Her mother had remarried and so my mum not only had natural siblings but also step brother and sisters. I do not think she accepted them as equals because whilst she was Labour supporting and passionate about fairness, she was just a bit of a snob. We sometimes had words about this.

It was always a given that her sons were better than other local kids. Whenever we talked about other families, it was always clear that approval went to those who we describe today as aspirational. Owen seemed to be in an especially talented class in his primary school and where we knew Labour councillors, they too seemed driven to help those who wanted to get on. I suppose it was equality of opportunity rather than social equality that was valued at the time amongst people who would not have described themselves as anything but working class.

In the early 1950s the Labour controlled London County Council had a scheme to send children from state primary schools to well-known London public schools. Owen went to Dulwich College. There cannot ever have been a more devoted Alleynian. My parents were rightfully proud and dad eventually went to watch Owen play first XV rugby. The school nurtured in him a passion for the RAF and he had a long and distinguished career in the service. Again, I fancy he found security in a structured and regimented environment, which as it happens, I could never have done.

Owen's career in the RAF began at the college at Henlow where he passed out with the 'sword of honour,' which meant he was the top student. I only wondered how a sword was appropriate to military aircraft.

Mum was expected to sit at the top table at the reception and spent weeks reading books on etiquette despite my advice that it was only the RAF not the Grenadier Guards.

Really, she deserved this day of glory. Her life had its frustrations. She told me that as a child she had won a scholarship to attend a grammar school in west London but never took the place. Like many others in the first half of the twentieth century, her working life scarcely reflected her aptitude and her daily life fell far short of her cultural aspirations. Her interests were not my dad's interests. She did not want to go off to race courses and she really hated going up the club on a Saturday evening. What she would like to have done is to go to a London theatre, not to see a show but to see some creative drama.

She first pushed me to read John Osborne and Arnold Wesker in the late 1950s. We listened to the 1958 Wesker Trilogy on the radio. This included *Roots,* about the cultural transformation through education of a farm labourer's daughter. This followed soon after the publication of Richard Hoggart's *Uses of Literacy,* which focussed on the influence of art, literature, and media on working class life. Later I took very seriously an academic work in 1962 by Jackson and Marsden, *Education and the Working Class* that tracked the lives of a group of socially mobile young people. It suggested that social mobility for working class families depended on selection to grammar schools, and that this created a new social divide.

These were part of the early sixties zeitgeist and things I could at least discuss with my mum who was an able and intelligent woman who spent too much time clearing up after us at home or folding people's sheets in the shop.

Without a father figure, I was lucky to have two such older brothers, Owen, and Jim. Until my early teens, life at home was stimulating and fulfilling.

Owen was a driven human being. He could be overly energetic and competitive. He was always in search of new and difficult things to do and had to do them as well as possible. He was a challenge and a challenger. He added to the family sense of high expectations encouraged by our parents. As soon as I showed an interest in cricket, he helped, throwing balls for me to hit, and allowing me to bowl at him and his friend from Dulwich College. Our musical tastes for many years were Owen's, Johnny Ray, and Frankie Laine at first, and we all had to listen to the *Goon Show*.

Jim was not like Owen. Closer in age, he was more of a pal and more available. He took me to things like the Biggin Hill air show or motor racing at Brands Hatch. If we were out in a crowd, he was physically protective, always putting his arm on my shoulder.

In February 1956 we went to an FA Cup match between Charlton Athletic, who I now supported, and Arsenal, or as they said in our parts 'The Arsenal' as the club had started in our own Woolwich Arsenal. A crowd of 71,000 turned up and the vast east terrace was heaving. Having arrived early, I left the terrace to go down to the shockingly inadequate toilets near the entrance. When I tried to return it was impossible. There was no way through, the pathways were blocked. Charlton's Valley Ground was one of the worst appointed in the old Division one and all I could do is scramble on to a bank and follow the game through the joyous and disheartening cries of nearby Arsenal fans. Tapscott and Bloomfield scored to put them 2-0 up at half time. At half time the crowd thinned out and I got back to Jim who was in a state of panic for my safety. There was no Charlton recovery. At one point the bookmakers had made them favourites to win the cup. That has never happened since. I have recently used google to find a Pathe News video of the game. Soft goals!

I first went down to the Valley at the end of the summer holidays in 1954. A home alone nine-year-old with nothing to do, I summoned some pocket money and caught the bus to Charlton, notwithstanding my view then that cricket was an infinitely better sport than football. Charlton beat Huddersfield Town two-one with goals from Kiernan and Ayre. I spent the whole evening reading and re-reading the match programme and in the years that followed I could recall every result plus scorers. I have been a supporter now for sixty-nine years, sharing anxieties, disappointments, despair, and isolated spots of elation with many others. Whether in Chicago, Burlington Vermont, the Southern Atlantic, the Norfolk Hotel in Nairobi, the Simla Hills in India, the Ocean Road in Australia, in a bungalow in Kenya, or in Paris, Rome or Barcelona, I have always gone to extraordinary lengths to find out the Charlton score. When they returned to the Valley in December 1992 I wept. If we look closely inside football clubs, they are not always the most attractive businesses and yet millions of us identify with a single team at a profound emotional level. In the early 1950s there was a greater sense that your local team was in some respects local. Quite a few of the players were from the Charlton area and if there were a few South Africans they too came to belong locally. Some Charlton players then also played cricket for Kent whilst others played local club cricket in south east London and north west Kent.

For many well-known individuals it seems to be de rigueur to have an identity team. Some politicians are passionately sincere about that: Roy Hattersley (Sheffield Wednesday), Ed Balls (Norwich City) Keir

Starmer (Arsenal) and before them Michael Foot (Plymouth Argyle). Others, perhaps have simulated a little. David Cameron seemed to be a bit confused on message as to whether his team was Aston Villa or West Ham, whilst Tony Blair claimed Jackie Milburn of Newcastle as his favourite player, despite the awkward fact that he could never have seen him play.

In my primary school days Charlton were a first division side (what is called the Premiership today) and had been there since 1936. Because of that I have always felt it an aberration that they have spent so much time since in lower divisions. In those early days, they used from time to time to win handsomely at home. In my first dedicated season they beat Aston Villa six-one, with South African Eddie Firmani scoring five, and Everton five-nil. The most memorable match however occurred at Christmas 1955.

On Boxing Day, they played the brilliant all conquering Manchester United 'Busby Babes' at Old Trafford. I spent most of the day waiting for sports report on the BBC Light programme. People as old as me will recall, perhaps, that sports report then used to allow good journalists to broadcast full interesting reports on matches and not waste our time on cliché ridden interviews with players and managers. So, I was alarmed to hear that the Busby Babes had outplayed Charlton and won five-one. But I was also interested to work out from the report that the manager had omitted five regulars from the normal strongest side.

The players of both sides shared a train down to London for the return the following day, their third match in four days on a heavy pitch. 41,340 spectators turned up including Owen and me and we saw Charlton inflict a three-nil defeat on Manchester United, their biggest of the season. Smart manager, Jimmy Seed, because his effective concession of the Old Trafford match had paid off at the Valley as fresh Charlton players had the stamina to run riot in the second half. Gauld and Ryan scored and their centre half put through his own goal.

~

Just over a year later, having dispensed with the services of Jimmy Seed, Charlton were hurtling towards relegation and on Monday 18 February played an early afternoon match again with Manchester United. I was able to get into the ground at half time on my way home from school. United were already three-nil up.

Predictable disappointment was balanced in the second half by the sight of a United player I had never heard of. What excited me most about Bobby Charlton was his passing in the Charlton half, powerful, direct, and incredibly accurate. He also completed his hat trick. I really believe he is the greatest English footballer I have seen in all these years. England would not have won the World Cup in 1966 without him, nor Manchester United the European Cup in 1968.

With Jim, it was possible to share mutual disappointments. We used to talk for hours across bedroom walls. In his mid-teens he used to turn out faithfully for a local cricket team. I went along and every Saturday I would hope that Jim would score some runs but he never really did. I have played cricket with a lot of people who enthusiastically appear week after week, look the part and shape up as if they know what they are about; but never enjoy personal success. Jim's cricket was a bit like that and I felt for him. Later I went to watch him play rugby and while waiting in the bar I heard the opposition saying what a good player Jim was. I was so pleased.

My mum used to recount two apparently significant aspects of my birth. The first was that I entered the world at the precise moment that a V-1 bomb, or as she called it a doodlebug, hit our streets in Abbey Wood. With the Woolwich Arsenal and the London Docks nearby, we were an inevitable target. At the edge of Bostall Woods we had had barrage balloons throughout the war. For years after the concrete bases from which the cables had been attached were spread across an open grass area. The other observation was that my birth was a marginal disappointment, as having had two boys my mum anticipated that there was a good chance of my being a girl. Elizabeth had been chosen as a name and I only became a Roger as an afterthought.

Decided in a rush, there was no time for a second Christian name. Many years later I was teaching a class of fifth formers (now year 11) and having watched a staff football match, they knew my Christian name but to avoid the work I had set they showed an unnecessary interest in my other Christian names.

As it was a history lesson, I explained to them about shortages and rationing at the end the Second World War and how my parents had only been allowed one Christian name.

After a serious pause for reflection, one of them said,

'you are kidding'?

We did not get a television until 1956, so I associate much of my home life until then with BBC radio. I do not think we can overstate the value of the radio to the quality of family life in the years after the war, or, of course, in the war itself. News, sport, and light entertainment were all of a high and intelligent standard. We had the *Goons* every week but the greatest of many good comedy programmes was the radio version of *Hancock's Half Hour*. We always had on *Any Questions,* still a vastly superior experience to the frequently egregious TV Question Time, plays on a Saturday night and *Paul Temple* on a Sunday evening. By the age of eleven, I had clocked up hours of cricket commentaries.

I also spent many hours following the 1955 general Election on the radio. I had attended a public meeting in my primary school where the Labour and Conservative candidates Christopher Mayhew and Henry Crawford had spoken courteously and answered questions.

Mayhew won the Woolwich East seat with sixty-four per cent of the vote.

The next year I attended another public meeting in Woolwich Town Hall, following the Suez crisis where the Conservative prime minister Anthony Eden ordered an invasion of Egypt in the grossly mistaken belief that the United States would sanction it. I was the only eleven years old there and was slightly alarmed at the vicious response of both local Tories and Labour to a poor man from the East Wickham Liberal Party who froze when he got up to speak.

I was genuinely interested in politics and found the details of election results almost as fascinating as the details of a cricket match. However, it was to be a long time before this interest manifested itself in serious participation.

If we wanted to watch TV, we could go to my nan's in Plumstead. It was there that I saw the Matthews Cup Final and the Coronation of the Queen. From time to time, we witnessed the *Flower Pot Men*, a party piece for comic imitation, with Owen and Jim as Bill and Ben and me relegated to weed.

Holidays were frugal and occasional. The four of us (not dad) went to Minster, a village in Thanet near the Kent coast. I was fascinated by the stilted politeness in the guest house breakfast room; such deference in the exchange of things like milk, sugar, or sauce for the sausages. Conversations were built on enquiries about where people had come from and which of our splendid Kent resorts people had visited during their stay.

'Have you been to Minnis Bay'?

'Oh, yes, it is very nice there. So quiet and not commercialised'

'That's so true, and isn't Birchington nice'?

'Oh exactly, I do so love Birchington.'

'Mind you, Margate and Ramsgate have their place and Broadstairs has a special feel to it, with Dickens and that sort of thing.'

It was a bit like the discussion between Hancock and Hugh Lloyd in the *Blood Donor*.

'Nice man that. Good conversationalist. Nice man (pause and then strident complaint) He's walked off with my wine gums. If you can't trust a blood donor, who can you trust'?

Thanet was very popular in the 1950s and from Minster we could catch a bus to several different resorts. We would go out all day and then return in the evening to mix with local youngsters on the village recreation ground. These were great evenings, only interrupted one night by a visit to the theatre in Ramsgate. The highlight was a performance of the *Laughing Policeman*, which did not require extraordinary talent but easily pleased a seven-year-old.

There was one memorable holiday. Dad had a half-sister called Barbara Willis. Only a little over five feet tall, she was married to the village baker in Haverhill in Suffolk and they had had thirteen children, and the family was quite a presence in the village, fast turning into a town with re-settlement from London after the war. Auntie Barb was a Labour Councillor. I always found her a remarkably calming person to be with. We had been on short trips to Haverhill before and I understand someone had driven down from London to Haverhill during a blackout during the war. There were always long and serious debates about the best railway route to take, either via Cambridge or changing at Audley End. I remember one journey from Cambridge to Haverhill on a train that probably had not advanced a lot from Stephenson's Rocket. So, one summer we stayed in Haverhill through most of August and the greatest fun was at harvest, running behind the combine harvester and chasing the rabbits disturbed by the massive machine.

Haverhill had their cricket team too and we followed them on a Saturday afternoon.

Did we ever have a holiday with dad? Well not really. His personal view was that if you spend several months at sea, a trip to a coastal town is a bit uninviting.

Even so, he did take Mum, Jim, and me to Brighton in June 1957, for three days. We went there without any booked accommodation, walked around for several hours, and eventually found somewhere to stay in Hastings Road. The three days had been carefully selected to coincide with three days horse racing on the downs. That was to be my mum's holiday, whilst Jim and I, said to be there on sufferance, were to spend three days watching Sussex play Northamptonshire at the County Cricket Ground at Hove. I still have a mental image of Don Smith bowling for Sussex from the sea end, left arm over medium pace with an elegant curving run up and rhythmic delivery. In my late teens I also had the opportunity to bowl from the sea end at Hove and even later I worked along with Don Smith on a cricket coaching course for England Under 15s.

My dad's brother lived in Brighton. Known in our family as the oldest teenager in Britain he introduced us to a good restaurant in the town. His name was Ernie but he did not like that. He did not like Truelove much either so we discovered when called to eat that we were out with Mr Charles True. We ate steak every night and I ate mushrooms for the first time.

Strangely, dad was happy enough to go on a boat trip down the Thames to Margate, but that was organised by the club. In the 1950s pleasure cruiser journeys used to run from Greenwich to Margate on a splendid vessel called the Royal Sovereign. We travelled down past Woolwich, Gravesend, and Sheerness through a part of Kent that feels so very different from other parts of the county, the Tunbridge Wells, Sevenoaks and Maidstones. Margate itself was a great attraction to Londoners with its fine beach and legendary Dreamland Playground. Every year one of the Working Men's clubs organised a day trip for at least a thousand children and it was every year a matter of continual enquiry in the street as to who had got on the Maybloom outing.

About thirty-forty coaches were lined up in Abbey Wood at 6.30 in the morning on a Thursday in July. Each coach was in a numbered order and it was pressed on us repeatedly that we must remember our coach number. The number became a matter of group identity and pride, anticipated in advance by constant discussion of which coach we were allocated to. One year our coach broke down and we lost our place in the numerical stream, something that impacted on our collective pride. So once the coach had recovered its will to travel, we all insisted that the driver should seek to restore us to our rightful place, and he did, recklessly overtaking down the dangerous Thanet way until we had restored our pride. No-one would do that now with a coach load of children. Nor should they!

These working men's clubs were an important part of London life. Most of the men also belonged to trade unions and people shopped principally in the co-op, known there as the Royal Arsenal Co-Operative Society. There was a social infrastructure that fostered support for the Labour Party and the Woolwich East seat which existed from 1918-1983 was held continually by Labour apart from a brief period in 1921 when a Tory supporting miner won a by election from Ramsay McDonald. In the 1950s Ernest Bevin represented the constituency for a year to be followed by Sir Christopher Mayhew who eventually, moved to the Liberal Party in 1974. When I joined my dad's club in the 1960s, I swore to back the ideas and values of the Labour Party. I suspect by that time, my support for that was more genuine than others, many of whom saw the club as a good drinking place and whose views in the bar were far from progressive.

For my mum, living in an exclusively male household, worse arrived when Owen joined a local cricket club. In the years after the war, a lot of people played cricket, and whether in the private clubs, the company grounds, or the public parks, they played seriously and properly. The club Owen joined played on several well-maintained public park pitches in south east London and my word, they took it seriously. And so did we! All through the week, the only topic of discussion through the summer was whether Bostall Sports had the right captain, what the batting order should be, whether the new man was really any use and whether the team had honestly demonstrated an appropriate will to win.

I can remember my outlook on life at that time, say from the age of seven to eleven. I was very secure and very self-confident. In school I was successful academically, I was captain of both the football and cricket teams, Head Boy and spoke in French at the School Prize Day. I also appeared on stage in the District Boy Scouts Gang Show. I was used to things going my way.

My closest friend during my Primary school years was Peter, only son of Arthur and Ethel Gray, who lived at the bottom of our road, at the King's Highway end. Arthur Gray believed in neighbourliness, in a very serious principled rather than gregarious way. So, with my mum being a quasi-single mum who had to work, I was frequently invited round to the Gray's, including for regular meals. Mrs Gray did not work. I do not think Arthur would have believed in that. He worked out of the London Transport Bus Garage in Plumstead, usually as a ticket inspector but sometimes as conductor. If mum and I got on one of Mr Gray's buses, he ensured we did not pay. He did this in a discreet way but, if this makes any sense, it was a rather ostentatious form of discretion, acting out the notion that he had not seen us in a very obvious way.

Peter was very proud of his dad as a cricketer. The bus drivers and conductors used to have some lovely Sunday trips with their families deep into the Kent countryside, to play all day cricket matches. One would drive the bus and the others would be free to drink the evenings away. Eventually, and much to my delight, I was invited along to a few matches. I can only remember one ground. It was at Boughton Monchelsea just south of Maidstone.

There was something very 1950s about this. Wives and children committed to following their men into the Kent countryside, a lot of conviviality with sport played seriously but fairly.

I never said this to Peter Gray, but his dad was not actually a good cricketer, though he took the game very seriously. He was one of those players who bats low in the order and bowls a couple of overs, after the main bowlers have finished.

But I did really share Peter's pride much later in 1962 when Arthur stood for the Woolwich Council in our Winn's Common ward. He was very much on the left of the Labour Party, and as was expected, he was easily elected with over 60% of the vote. Sadly, he only served once. He did not care for the way Labour Councillors shared friendships with members of the Conservative party and by the end complained that it was impossible to tell them apart. Arthur was not a very flexible man. After the 11+ Peter went to a different Secondary school and I saw less of the Grays, apart from Mr Gray's election to the Council.

~

Our local Primary School was called Bostall Lane when Jim and Owen attended, a good name because it was in the lane leading up to Bostall Woods. But by the time I went there it was called Alexander McLeod, after someone of repute in the co-op movement but meaning little to our community. Changing school names has a long and pointless history. The other local school fondly known as Purrett Road, became a grand Galleons Mount.

The ground from the marshes by the river Thames rises quite steeply to the top of Bostall Woods and the school was on high ground. It was a large primary school, three storeys high and with four classes in each age group. From a classroom at the top of the school, we could see for miles and I can remember looking at the Great Flood of 1953, the passage of the Royal Yacht Britannia up the river and quite alarmingly a plane crashing into the Royal

31

Arsenal in September 1953. There was a very large playground, where I broke my left arm in two places in a football match, spending the next six months in plaster. In the final year before secondary school, we used to go to the top of the playground, nearest the woods, to play football after school on a Friday. For a few weeks a small group of girls came to watch and then persuaded me to join them in the woods for some round robin snogging. This did not last too long. It was different when my friend Alan Cooper had a party at his house in Federation Road near the school, organised by his widowed mum.

Mrs Cooper had arranged an equal number of boys and girls to attend and then initiated a sort of lottery to pair up a boy and a girl for a brief kiss outside the living room door. I was quite enthusiastic about the game if the lottery paired me up with Angela Mann. There were times when I believed I adored Angela Mann. She was learning ballet and I liked her not just for her pretty face but also for the pretty way she walked.

Well, we were paired up. We went outside but she asked me if we could avoid doing what we were supposed to do. Lamely I agreed. Who knows how she might have responded if I had told her how desperately disappointed, I was? It was not to be the only wasted opportunity in the years ahead. The fear of rejection is so powerful, at least for some of us.

~

That was the year, 1956, when we took the divisive 11+ I was allocated a grammar school place. I did not get the first-choice school that we opted for and ended up at one of the more unfashionable grammar schools in south east

London. For a time, this was regarded as a disaster and for several years my mum would blame the school for any shortcomings I might have had as a teenager. Located in Deptford, Addey and Stanhope Grammar that year recruited pupils throughout south east London and I had friends from places as diverse as Beckenham and Eltham. In retrospect, I do not regret at all that I did not go to one of the more popular and more academically successful schools. The school is part of my profile and the fact that I was only the third student to go to Oxford University is part of my story. I went through the school in a class of able pupils and I would not have wanted never to know Stephen Wealthall, David Quinlan, and George Challand. Of these Stephen Wealthall had his difficult moments. On one occasion he drew the school on to the front page of the local paper, the South East London Mercury, by barricading himself with suitable armaments from the woodwork room in preparation for an expected assault from some less intelligent members of the school. On another occasion, he enraged our very mild-mannered form master, Mr Howls, by bringing locally produced fascist leaflets into the school. Stephen was about the only one in the class from Deptford but he took his world view from his grandfather in Doncaster. From beginning to end he said he was going to be a doctor. He duly qualified at the School of Medicine at Sheffield University, researched into cot death at the Nuffield Institute in Oxford, became Fulbright Fellow in Cleveland Ohio, returned to Sheffield to lecture in Child Health and then became Director of Medical Education at the University of Auckland. His death from lung cancer in July 2015 was reported in the *New Zealand*

33

Herald under the headline 'We knew the time was coming' *Death of Stephen Wealthall*, the doctor who taught us not to fear the end.

I was lucky to be taught by intelligent and culturally refined teachers, especially, Mr Dawson, Mrs French, and Mr Checksfield, who to my surprise advised me to go to Oxford. In other schools I would not have been picked out and encouraged in that way.

Unlike all the other grammar schools on offer in south east London, Addey and Stanhope had one distinct advantage. It was a co-educational school and, as above, I would not have wanted never to have known Gillian Feaver, Lorna Davison, and Jennifer Courtney, each of whom I remember fondly in different ways. It was a shame, at that time, that so few of the more able girls stayed on to the sixth form and instead went off to do girls' jobs below their real potential. The mood at this school was a kindly, even genteel one. As a three-form entry school with a small sixth form, the teaching staff were tightknit, loyal, and apparently good friends who enjoyed each other's company. Mr Checksfield and his wife took a small group of us out to London one Saturday and for the first time I ate pizza. There was a lot of good extra -curricular things going on, such as speaking competitions in both English and French, and a music one too. There was an annual school production in the nearby Greenwich Town Hall and every morning the music master played a piece of classical music and gave us a short talk on the composer and his style. I remember telling my dad all about Sibelius.

In the sixth form I was allowed to do my own full school

assemblies. Perhaps, had we had key stage tests and constant attainment targets we might have hit some higher academic targets but would we really have been better educated? As my brief account of Dr Stephen Wealthall suggests it is often about nurturing potential rather than driving youngsters through premature hurdles.

Naturally, we only had half the number of boys available to compete in boys only competitive sport against other schools. Our age group did very well. As an Under fifteen football team, we went through autumn and winter terms undefeated and we won quite a lot of cricket matches.

Playing for the school was time consuming. My home was at least one and a half hour's bus journey from our playing field at Downham, near Bromley. Sometimes we travelled further say to John Ruskin in Croydon, where Roy Hodgson the football manager was at school. I used to travel from Abbey Wood with John Rooke, a devoted Charlton Athletic supporter who ended up being the boot boy for the first team when they were in the Premier Division.

On a November Saturday in 1959 we made the great trek out to Croydon on the 54 bus and got a two-all draw in an Under 15 match with Ruskin. It took us two hours to get back as far as Woolwich and all the way home we speculated on how Charlton had got on at Aston Villa. No phone updates then, but we knew we could get a Saturday evening results paper at our journey's end. As soon as he saw a pile of the then pink papers on the corner of Wellington Street, John flew off the bus, bought the paper and passed it to me when I caught up. At first, I thought it said one-all. But it did not. Villa had won eleven-one. As we caught the onward bus to Abbey Wood, we agreed that the two-all draw at Ruskin had been a good result.

Sometimes we played our matches in the morning and if Charlton were away, I used to pass lonely Saturday afternoons just hoping that the Charlton match would be featured on the BBC second half radio commentary. In those days the rules dictated that they could only cover one match and they had to select from all four divisions so there was about a two per cent chance of Charlton being on. Nor were they allowed to advertise which match was being covered until they joined the commentary team at half time. It was a moment of anticipation where hope was always dashed. Until finally in September 1959 they announced 'we are now going to Boothferry Park for a Second Division match between Hull City and Charlton Athletic.' The commentator who was called Maurice Edelston, then announced the score as Hull nil Charlton two, which by full time had become nil-four, with two goals for Summers, and one each for Lawrie and Leary. Edelston did not seem at all impressed. A former professional footballer, whose father had played for Hull, he was more focussed on the shortcomings of the home side.

This was Charlton's third season in the second division having been relegated in 1957. Many of us had held out confident hopes that they would return in the following season. In December 1957, I went down to the Valley on a miserable afternoon for one of the most extraordinary matches ever played against Bill Shankley's

Huddersfield Town. Charlton lost their skilful captain Derek Ufton in the seventeenth minute, taken to hospital with a dislocated shoulder. There were no substitutes then and with their numerical superiority, and a good side, 'Town' were five-one up with less than thirty minutes left. Charlton won seven-six. With ten minutes left they were six-five in the lead but conceded an equaliser, only to go back and score a seventh. It is the stuff of legend that the Charlton forward, Johnny Summers tried out some new boots at half time and despite being left footed, scored five goals with his right foot, some of them quite spectacular, though with a little assistance from the slightly theatrical Huddersfield keeper.

As that season ended, I went with friends to the penultimate match away at Ipswich Town. I think Ipswich had only become a professional club in the late 1930s and their ground was charmingly rustic. We stood on a mud bank where locals positioned the small stools, they had brought with them. The stands were low and we could see trolley buses going past all afternoon. However, there were still over 20,000 crammed in the ground and Ipswich, with Alf Ramsey as manager, were about to move up to higher things and the League First Division title in 1963.

In truth, they were the better side. They wasted chances and allowed Charlton to score on the break. Our side won four-one, totally against the run of play. It now meant a draw at home to Blackburn in the last game would secure promotion back to the top division. Blackburn won four-three. It was a signal moment in the steady decline of my team.

By this time both my brothers had left home to join the RAF and compared with my primary school years, I did find home life lonely at times. I cherished time playing club cricket at Dartford and I spent a little time as a colt at a professional football club, actually scoring against Charlton. I gave that up when they started to teach me some of the unfair tricks of professional football.

My mid-teens saw some behavioural aberrations. Climbing out of the window during detention led to an unfulfilled threat of caning from the headmaster, who likewise was not pleased when his important delegation of visitors found us kicking rolled up aprons around the playground during a woodwork lesson. I doubt whether the woodwork teacher got commended either but he was generally pleased not to have me in the room. I once asked him truculently why some boys got mahogany and others only got oak.

'If I had my way Truelove, you wouldn't get orange boxes to play with,' said Mr Turnage.

I caused perpetual problems for a young Welsh woman teacher, who took us for geography and biology in the third year. It does not matter that she was Welsh, but I do recall her voice and accent which stridently betrayed her frustrations with me. Week after week, I was sent out of lessons to stand in the corridor or wander off round the school. She sent me out once for 'making eyes at her.'

The fact was her lessons were rotten. In geography we were supposed to be studying the United States. That could have been interesting but instead of proper teaching, lesson after lesson consisted of dictated notes, raw and meaningless, with no question-and-answer analysis, no discussion, no explanation, and no reflection. I saw no point in this and kept interrupting the dictated flow with supercilious and supposedly funny comments until I got dismissed. I borrowed others' notes and at the end of the year came top and was presented with the school prize for geography. That still does not justify this lack of proper teaching which in fact has always been too prevalent in our grammar schools, as my children all found out much later.

In the sixth form of the school, I began to do a bit more than sport and found the A levels in history and English far more interesting than O level learning. I also did Latin but with little enthusiasm. For history I relied a lot on reading books by AJP Taylor, a popular but controversial historian in the early 1960s. I read several Thomas Hardy novels, some nineteenth century French novels by Stendhal, Flaubert and Zola in translation and Americans like Norman Mailer and Sinclair Lewis. I read Royal Court type plays, the Shakespeare tragedies and I went to a church in London to see TS Eliot's *Murder in the Cathedral*.

One of our A level English teachers was Mrs French, the Deputy Head who terrified most of us and whose lessons I first entered with trepidation. She was very good at interpreting the physiognomy of Chaucer's pilgrims in the *Prologue to the Canterbury Tales*. One day in her office I noticed a book on her shelf which I then got from the public library. This was the source of her erudition and with its help, and without over exploiting it, I was able to match her for perceptive comments on the appearance of the Canterbury travellers.

However, it was our kindly History teacher who in the autumn of 1962 suggested I should have a go at getting into Oxford, specifically into St Edmund Hall. Mr Checksfield was a man I really liked and looked up to. He was cultured, civilised and humane, and not withstanding that he was a good cricketer, whose son played for Oxford University in a first -class match with Leicestershire. I think we pursued my application as a speculative idea but good experience. We were not banking on it.

On a Monday morning at the beginning of December 1962, I made my way to Oxford and to St Edmund Hall, at the bottom of the High Street. Some of my actions that week were more Mr Bean than potential Oxford undergraduate. The first night I was given a room. I sat in front of the fire and revised some British history until I felt tired. Looking round the room I saw no bed. Perhaps it was hidden in the cupboard. It was not, however many times I opened it. This was obviously some kind of discrimination. The next morning, I found a college servant and he showed me my bedroom for the week on the next floor. The next morning, I took an exam paper and then after lunch set out for the town centre only for a helpful fellow applicant to tell me we had an afternoon paper to do. As it happened it was Ancient Greek and the examiners were happy for us to exempt ourselves if we had never learnt any Greek. On the Wednesday evening I could not find the tutor's room for the key interview and had to be traced and brought forward for a slightly truncated exchange.

Undaunted I was getting on with the entrance papers. I enjoyed doing two history papers but also relished the general paper and the three-hour extended essay. The first asked an eclectic mix of chattering class questions on drama, politics, literature and media and the Special Essay gave us a choice between Opportunism or Pressure Groups.

I opted for the latter and wrote almost entirely about how the Labour Party from 1900-1918 was a pressure group rather than a political party, something cribbed from a book by Henry Pelling.

My school thought I had gone for a one-day interview not a week. On the Friday they rang my mum to ask where I was and with extra urgency because they wanted me for a first eleven football match the following morning.

We were playing Bromley Technical School, where David Bowie went to school and it was nearly two hours from home.

The week in Oxford had been good. I liked being there and came back with a bit of extra self-esteem. They had obviously had a problem getting the team together because the first eleven that we put on the pitch was the first nine and one of the nine had forgotten his boots and turned out in his ordinary shoes. It was decided we would pack our defence whilst I stayed up front and if we got the ball, they would hammer it in my direction. We won five-four. I scored four and provided a tap in for the fifth.

The following Saturday I got a letter from St Edmund Hall. It offered me a place to read History at Oxford University. Sublime!

In the months ahead I worked so hard with so much

incentive. A few weeks before we took our exams David Quinlan came in with the news that his father had died. I thought what an awful shock for him and did not know what to say.

Then one Friday evening I got home from school and was surprised to find the front door open. I went in and found my mum who had clearly been dead for some hours. I sprinted to the local doctors. I asked our neighbours for help and the rest of our family were informed and my dad flown back from around the world.

The previous Sunday mum had fallen in the garden and had been suffering pain. I had told her to go to the hospital but I had not insisted strongly enough. She had broken a rib and it had punctured her lung. I had bad dreams about this for several years and still feel guilt.

To lose your mum at the age of only fifty-seven is a sad and painful experience, especially when you feel it might have been avoidable, and you might have made it avoidable. It had a destabilising impact for some time. From the time my brothers left to join the RAF, and my father spent most of his life at sea, my mum and I perforce spent many hours, days, and years together. These were my teenage years and I did not always feel as truly grounded as I once had. My mum was not especially averse to rehearsing her disappointments with life, which were twofold; then I only partly appreciated the negative sense that a woman partially abandoned must feel but there was always a problem of an adult human being unfulfilled in many other ways.

I did not always appreciate the complaints. I had my own adolescent issues too. I do not like to think I have been unsympathetic to women with legitimate causes to moan, but generally I do not prefer the long version.

My mum never knew I got the A levels and went to Oxford. She would really have enjoyed visiting me there, I am sure. No book on etiquette would have been necessary. I often thought about this over the next four years. I would have found it a profound support had she been around.

The summer after mum died was a difficult one. Somehow, I did not want to be at home. For a time, I went off to school camp and then for the rest of the summer I kept journeying down to Haverhill in Suffolk on my scooter. In between I would travel back to play cricket for Kent and London Under 19s and for my club Dartford. These travels came to an end one Sunday evening when I put my cricket kit and my fellow opening bowler on the back of the Lambretta and set off for the Gravesend Jazz Club. We got as far as Pepper Hill when the back tyre exploded and to save us from colliding with the passing cars, I turned the scooter on to the footpath. The bike was a write off and I have had a lifelong scar on my left elbow. We went to a hospital rather than the Jazz Club and until I went off to Oxford I stayed at home.

It was not long before dad sold 97 Bastion Road and bought a flat nearer the club. He died of old age in 1982. My brothers both died prematurely, Jim in 1997 and Owen in 2006. I delivered the eulogy at Jim's funeral and spoke about Owen at a memorial service at Dulwich College. They were hard things to do but I kept my composure and was determined to get the message right. Of Jim I said how proud I was of him, of his term of office as Mayor of Dover Town, of his rugby and his sailing. I also said that he could be a brilliantly funny, but like so many funny people, he could have his moments of sadness and doubt. At Dulwich I spoke of Owen's pride at being an Alleynian, his drive and competitiveness, his sense of adventure but also his sensitivity. They had both made my early life so much more exciting than most. They were both men of character and energy. They also had strong opinions, but that is a whole family trait.

Thus, I am the only one of five members of my first nuclear family still alive.

I have such a clear memory of things in my early life and it would be nice sometimes to share a thought or two with someone who could share that memory, but I cannot.

3

YOUNG CRICKETER

It was Friday 20 June 1952, so I was seven years old. Jim picked up our local paper, the Kentish Independent, and announced there was a cricket match the following day, between Kent and Surrey at the Rectory Field Blackheath. It was decided that we should go.

It was a memorable day. I was truly enchanted. It is an unattractive urban cricket ground but I loved every minute. We sat opposite the pavilion and its clock and I phased the movement of the score on the board with the movement of the clock, and realised that cricket is a slow-moving story with a perpetually changing plot. At least, it was then. Built into the emerging stories are constant assessments of time. I found it fascinating to calculate the change in runs and wickets over half hour intervals, as in between three and three-thirty Kent made twenty for one wicket. It is the uncertainty of outcome and a subtle balance between personal and team performance that attracts so many to the game.

At tea we were let on to the ground. Only seven years since the war, there were many men of military gait who marched authoritatively out to the middle to inspect the wicket. They probably did not deduce much, but it was part of the scene.

By tea Kent had been bowled out for 217. A lot of useful twenties and thirties the consensus around us agreed, which meant nobody had got as much as fifty. In those days Surrey was much stronger than Kent.

From then on, I supported both sides for a few years. At that time, it was usually a case of willing Surrey to win and hoping that Kent would not lose.

I read the cricket scores in the *News Chronicle* every day and listened to the lunchtime cricket scoreboard on BBC radio. In the evenings I could not wait for the close of play county cricket scoreboard. I wanted to see another county game and in August dad, no less, took Jim and me to the Oval for the return Surrey v Kent fixture. The Oval is a very different ground to Blackheath and again I was overwhelmed with excitement by the whole environment. We sat on the gasholder side, looking left to the grand pavilion and across the ground to the Archbishop Tenison's School and the buses going down the Harleyford Road. Surrey completed a double of victories but only by two wickets, having been held up by Kent's South African batsman Sid O'linn, who was also a Charlton wing half. In those days of bowler domination, sides had a fair number of scratchy strokeless players who just survived and nudged and nurdled their way to occasional hundreds and O'linn was one of these.

Apart from Blackheath, the Kent grounds were not accessible for a primary school boy from south east London, but the Oval was. I could get there and back by bus safely and so until I went to secondary school, the Oval was my favourite venue and I have been there frequently in recent years. I am reminded of those days of complete happiness.

The best days at the Oval were when Peter May scored a hundred, which was quite often. Writers have always focussed on May's leg side play but he could be very powerful through extra cover. Sometimes when they played on the gasholder side of the ground the boundary was a concrete wall. I can remember an innings against Glamorgan where the poor ball kept crashing into the extra cover boundary when May was batting at the pavilion end. By contrast with May's elegant power, I also liked the pragmatic style of Ken Barrington. My favourite Surrey bowler was not the destructive off spinner Jim Laker, nor left arm spinner Tony Lock, but the crab like and almost histrionic opening bowler Peter Loader, who in July 1953 came charging in from the rugby stand at Blackheath taking nine for twenty eight in sixteen overs as Kent were skittled for sixty-three.

It was a good time too to follow the England cricket team. After our family trip to the Oval in 1952, Jim and I followed up by going to the final Test match of the summer against India. The whole country seemed to be excited about a new fast bowler from Yorkshire called Trueman. At Headingly, he had reduced India to nought for four wickets and now in London he took five wickets and bowled India out for ninety eight. They were not the strong side they are today but they had some lovely exotic names like Ghulam Ahmed and Polly Umrigar.

1953 was a more serious year. England and Australia came to the last test at the Oval all square, after four drawn matches, the draw at Lord's only being secured through a heroic partnership between Watson and Bailey that had the whole country engrossed. On the third morning Jim and I got up very early and got to the ground about four hours before play was due to start at eleven-thirty. Jim was twelve and I was eight.

There were already massive queues and by the time we got through the entrance gate there were no seats left in the ground. We were allowed on to the grass to crouch for a whole day's cricket. I spent much of the day praying for wickets to fall so that we could stretch our legs. Happily, they did, frequently. England got a lead of thirty-one which in a series of low scores was a real advantage. Then through the afternoon session Australia were bowled out by the Surrey spinners Lock and Laker, in conditions that suited their bowling. By the end of the day England were well set to win, a task which was completed the following day with Compton hitting a four. There was great national joy and Jim and I were overwhelmed with pride that we had been there on that crucial day. Of course, I could not have had that honour without a brother who in those days opened so many exciting opportunities.

It was a privilege to be at the Oval for that decisive day. I can see now Laker from the pavilion end with his upright simple action and Lock from the Vauxhall end, aggressive in approach and delivery, and thought by some to be throwing rather than bowling his left arm spin. Actually, they did change ends, because Lock bowled Harvey from the pavilion end, and throwing or not, I found him an exciting competitor.

The winning of the Ashes was not the only moment of

national pride and unity that summer. In May the whole country, so it seemed, was drawn to what was known as the Matthews Cup Final, when Blackpool came from three-one down to beat Bolton Wanderers four-three, though Bolton were down to ten players. The country seemed together too as Hillary and Tensing conquered Everest, for the Coronation of the Queen and even for the horse Pinza winning the Derby at Epsom. A year later the sub four-minute mile was achieved by Roger Bannister at Iffley Road in Oxford.

These events around 1953 and 1954 were patriotically warming in a positive way.

By the end of November 1954, England were again playing Australia for the Ashes, starting with the first test in Brisbane. From then, until the beginning of March 1955, I spent many early mornings taking the radio to the kitchen and struggling to hear the commentary from Australia. The sound would come and go, there were continual background noises that seemed like the wind and waves from the oceans but it was possible, to an extent, to follow events. It was a famous series. England were annihilated at Brisbane but came back to win in Sydney, Melbourne, and Adelaide. They had experimented by taking a raw but very fast bowler from Northamptonshire, Frank Tyson, on tour and he dominated the series in a way he never repeated. There were also some great batting performances from Peter May and Colin Cowdrey.

By 1956, I was in my last few days in primary school and the summer was dominated by another Ashes series. On Friday 22 June I asked mum if I could miss school and go to the second test at Lord's. It was the first time I had been to Lord's, which is so much more refined than the Oval, as different as the garish colours of the MCC are different to the brown cap of Surrey. Australia was bowled out for 285. I have vivid memories of Trueman from the pavilion end knocking back Keith Miller's off stump and Statham from the Nursery end completely removing Peter Burge's middle stump.

England's reply was disappointing but memorable for Keith Miller, supposedly not fit to bowl, dismissing Richardson and Graveney in an explosive and probably courageous spell and then the introduction of their crablike tenacious batsman, Ken Mackay as a surprise bowler. Cowdrey drove a widish half volley towards the grandstand. The crowd all looked to the boundary only to see Richie Benaud very close in on the offside holding one of the great catches of all time.

Australia won the test but England retained the Ashes, thanks to Jim Laker taking nineteen wickets at Old Trafford, yet another occasion in the 1950s, when cricket appeared to unite the whole country. We were out playing cricket in the field at the back of our garden, and every time a wicket fell in the second innings an elderly neighbour woman, who was not generally very friendly, came out to let us know.

This series is, as said, always associated with Laker's nineteen wickets at Old Trafford, but he also took a few at Headingly too. What is not dwelt on, understandably, was the extraordinary success of the selectors. After defeat at Lord's, and conscious of some holes in the batting line up, they first selected one of their own Cyril

Washbrook, aged forty-one to play, and he made a decisive ninety-eight at Headingly in partnership with Peter May. Then they turned to an Anglican Minister, the first ordained minister to bat for England, and David Sheppard, later Bishop of Liverpool, made 113 at Old Trafford; and finally, a far from fit Denis Compton was brought back and scored ninety-four at the Oval.

The 1950s were really the days against which I have ever after judged the game of cricket: three Ashes wins, Surrey champions seven times and by 1960 Kent beginning to be a serious county side. By 1960 too I was playing first eleven cricket for a town club, and playing for Kent in schoolboy cricket.

By 1956, I was desperate to play some proper cricket, not in the field, the common or the beach, but formally on a prepared pitch, taking guard to bat, the umpire calling play and a scorebox and scoreboard in the corner of the ground.

I was in luck.

First, local primary school teachers in the borough of Woolwich organised a cricket league to be played on proper pitches on the borough's public parks. This was all in whites, eleven- a- side, hard ball, neat little scorebooks, and umpires in coats cricket.

Today initiation into cricket is more likely to be through kwik cricket which gives children the opportunity to carry on batting even when technically out and with a ball that does not hurt. In 1956 too many little boys, and it was boys only, had very short opportunities to bat, enjoyed little reward and sometimes had to hold back tears when hit by an unfamiliar hard ball. They knew no better then.

In the mid-1980s, I played for the MCC at Felsted School in Essex. I made runs and shared in a 150 opening partnership so the school cricket coach thought I was appropriate to talk to.

He was a former Essex opening batsman, Gordon Barker. I told him I had seen him bat at Gravesend in 1957 and sure enough he knew how many he had scored, how he was out and who had caught the catch. It transpired that he could recall in detail every first-class innings he had ever played. I played competitive cricket for nearly fifty years but I will only refer to some better days in this chapter, as most old cricketers generally do.

So, the first bit of success.

In the Woolwich primary league, we played one match against a school from Plumstead called Timbercroft. Team scores in such matches were naturally quite small and we bowled them out for twenty-eight and I took five wickets for two runs. When we batted, we were soon no runs for four wickets but still won by six wickets and I made twenty-nine not out.

When the exciting news emerged that Kent County Cricket club were going to set up what would now be called a centre of excellence, I was put forward on the basis of performances such as the one above and in October 1956 I started what turned out to be seven years of committed attendance at the centre in Eltham. Every Thursday throughout my youth I lugged a cricket bag around the school, left school promptly at three-forty ran up Tanners Hill to Lewisham Way and willed the number twenty-one bus to get to Eltham as soon as possible. The initiative by Kent was part of their steady improvement as a county club and it paid rich dividends in the years ahead. The driving force, I think, was John Pretlove, Assistant Secretary and a first-eleven player who had already played for Cambridge University. The coaches over the subsequent years came from Sittingbourne. There was Claude Lewis, a former left arm spinner, coach, future scorer, and owner of an antiques shop in East Street Sittingbourne. He was supported by Bob Wilson a stylish opening batsman and the third coach was a left arm spinner from Bapchild, called Brian Luckhurst, who eventually became a Test match opening batsman. The coaching sessions were frequently observed by the county manager Leslie Ames who did so much to transform Kent into a strong professional side.

Not unreasonably I started to go to watch Kent play rather than Surrey. I went to Gravesend, Gillingham, Maidstone, and Dartford.

I first went to the Bat and Ball at Gravesend in 1958 to see Kent play Essex. It was an easy train journey with a stroll up Wrotham Road where there is a house close to the ground where my dad grew up. Dad said he used to watch cricket at the Bat and Ball before the first world war, when Kent was a strong side. He could reel off the names of most of the side, which won the county championship in 1909 and 1910.

My Huish, Hutchings, and Humphreys long ago!

Inside the small Bat and Ball ground you can easily imagine you are back in Edwardian times. The ground is surrounded by Victorian and Edwardian terrace houses and at the north end there was an old workhouse. There was a large scoreboard in the north east corner of the ground, with a large grass bank in front, a natural habitat for the more raucous and least deferential spectators.

I went again two years later and saw Bob Wilson get an entertaining 145 against Worcestershire who had a strong opening attack of occasional England bowlers called Jack Flavell and Len Coldwell. I later played there for Kent Schools Under 19s against the MCC Young Professionals and for Dartford against Gravesend. During my student days I played regularly for Gravesend Wednesday. Clubs used to run mid-week sides, for people such as retail shop owners who closed early on Wednesdays but were open all day Saturday. It was also an opportunity for some quite elderly gentlemen to step out on to their much-loved field, the only cricketers I think I have played with who did not actually move when fielding other than for a stately change of position at the end of the over. Kent played the last of their 142 fixtures at the Bat and Ball in 1971. In the tight urban environment, there was too little room for cars and so the cricket week flags came down for the last time.

Then late in August 1958 I told mum that I was off to watch Kent play. She was used to my getting back about seven to eight o'clock in the evening and as a thirteen-year-old she was happy with that. But this was Dover, Kent v Middlesex. The hours of play were set from twelve to seven. After 7pm I got the bus from the Crabble Ground back to Dover Priory and then got a slow train to Gillingham. Well, it was after midnight before I got back to Woolwich Arsenal and the last bus had gone. I walked to Abbey Wood and got home about 1am. My mum had got the police out looking for me.

Also, in the summer of 1957, we were informed that the most promising youngsters at the Eltham nets would play an all-day match with a comparable group from Canterbury and the rest of East Kent. It was to be played at the St. Lawrence Ground at Canterbury which was a brilliant opportunity and reflected the seriousness with which the club was taking their youth development programme.

In those days Kent used to play their home matches all round the county and so there was room in the calendar to arrange young cricketer games on the county headquarters ground. Over the next seven years, I played there at least once every year, always bowling from the pavilion end, where the slope is thought to help away swing. I used to open the bowling, running in from fourteen paces, quite quick for my age until I tried to get clever and experiment with too many types of delivery.

On that August day in 1957, our team emerged from various railway routes in south east London and north Kent and joined forces to pick up a steam train at Chatham. As we travelled through what is now a familiar journey from Chatham to Faversham it simply poured with rain. Spirits were low. The train then pulled out of Faversham and by the time we got to Selling, the sky was blue, the sun was out and the rest of the day was perfect. From Canterbury East station we were marched up the Old Dover Road and were shown into the pavilion, told to change in the players dressing room and then as play began, we trooped out through the front pavilion door.

We lunched on the same tables as the first-class players, served by the same courteous staff. This was great. The opposition, many of whom were used to regular cricket at several prep schools, were better than us but we got a respectable score thanks to a boy from Catford, called John Copus, who later played for Surrey and then became a skilled bat maker.

These fixtures lasted for three years. The following year, my family decided to come and support me, mixing the day up with a trip into Canterbury for a lobster lunch. I was told after this match that I had bowled well and was unlucky not to take wickets but to my family I was thought to have failed in some respect.

To them, these matches were clearly some kind of trial and it was wildly bruited that I probably would not be invited back for the following winter.

The following week a return match was organised at the Lensbury and Britannic House Ground in Sydenham. My family said they would come along at tea time. When they arrived, I was able to tell them that this time we were winning and that I had largely bowled Canterbury out, taking eight for twenty.

I was told by my mum not to be boastful.

In the 1959 Kent Handbook I was listed as one of the three most promising youngsters in Kent, though that was only based on that one performance, I think.

This involvement with the Eltham centre, led easily to my playing in Kent Schools representative sides which I did for four years from under fifteen to under nineteen. In June 1960 we were lucky enough to play an all-day under fifteen county game on the St. Lawrence Ground against Essex Schools. By this time, Kent was the strongest schools' side in the south of England, with future Test cricketers like Alan Knott and Derek Underwood in the side plus two useful quick bowlers from Maidstone, David Sadler the future Manchester United centre half and Colin Fagg, the son of a past Kent opening batsman. In these sides I was not regarded as any kind of batsman and batting at number eleven, hit the first ball for six and the second was caught on the boundary. I did take the wickets of both opening batsmen but with so many good bowlers the subsequent wickets were shared and we won comfortably.

The same season, I can record one school match I played as an under fifteen but in the school first side. Somehow, we had got a fixture with Heath Clark Grammar School from Croydon, who fancied themselves a bit as a good cricket school. They turned up with a few Surrey young cricketers in their side and a teacher with a background in schools' representative cricket. I was pleased then as county number eleven for the under fifteens, to score sixty-three at number four for the school and then to take six for fifteen in what was an overwhelming victory helped in the bowling department by an enthusiastic Bert Trodd.

I remember two interesting Kent Schools matches in the next two years, because they were captained firstly by Derek Underwood and then secondly by Alan Knott, both to be future great England cricketers.

In 1961 we had an under sixteen game against London Schools at Hayes near Bromley. London Schools was a bit of an anomaly because all the players were technically eligible to play for other counties with county cricket clubs. London Schools Cricket Association had however strong roots in organising cricket for young people in London and I think Denis Compton had played for them before the second world war. In my last year in school, I played for both Kent and London under nineteens.

This day in Hayes was a good one for me personally, but it might have been better. I took four early wickets and was ready to try to run through their side. But the captain Derek Underwood kept wanting to take me off which in a competitive representative match seemed an odd tactic. At that point, before he joined the Kent staff, Derek Underwood was a quickish first change bowler, already remarkably effective and accurate. Once he had taken me off, he came on and took some wickets and we bowled London out for seventy.

Still 297 test wickers!

It was not expected to be a difficult task but then we saw this enormous boy marking out a very long run. He was called Geoff Arnold; he was also a young Surrey cricketer and he too was to be a fine England bowler. When I went in, this time at number ten, we were fifty for eight but we still managed to win by one wicket. I was not out. I had some difficulty locating the deliveries from Arnold and was hit on the head but also played some unexpected good shots.

Derek Underwood, of course, played for the Kent first team at a young age and we did not see anything of him in the under nineteen age group matches but Alan Knott did still play for the schools' side in 1962. He was such a talented all-round cricketer, from a strong cricketing family background in Belvedere. He did not live far away from me and so we often travelled together and I knew him well. An early topic of discussion was whether he wanted to be a wicket keeper or a bowler because in his early teenage years he was a very good off and leg spin bowler. He made the right choice and although there would be strong opposition as wicket keeper from others like Leslie Ames and Godfrey Evans, I would pick him in an all-time best Kent side, not least because he would be needed to keep to Underwood.

Just as we were lucky to play our youth cricket at the St Lawrence Ground in Canterbury, another highlight for me was playing on the Sussex County Ground at Hove. We had an under nineteen game in 1962 and Alan Knott was captain.

Quite clearly, he was not as keen as Derek Underwood to take me out of the attack as soon as I took wickets. Those familiar with Hove will know it is believed that bowling from the sea end helps bowlers who swing the ball and I guess the manager of our team had told Knott that I might be the most likely to do that. So, we started at half past eleven and I was still running up the hill and bowling when lunch arrived at half past one. Resuming just after two, I was asked to continue from the same end and was still in harness when the Sussex innings ended about an hour later. I had bowled for over three hours unchanged with quite a long run up. Our manager, Mr Pope said I was big hearted. In modern youth cricket that could not happen. There are tight limits on the length of spells that young quick bowlers can bowl, and the definition of quick includes some medium paced dib dob trundlers. The remarkable thing is that whilst everything is now done to protect young fast bowlers, those who progress to first class and test cricket do seem alarmingly prone to serious long-term injuries. What struck me, watching a first-class match last year, was how uniform the bowling actions were, as if they had all been coached to a template. When we look back at say Trueman, Statham, Tyson, Snow, Willis, and Gough, they all had distinctive actions, which possibly suited their bodies. They built their strength by bowling.

I took five wickets and Mr Pope, the manager, asked me to sign a form that nominated me for the English Schools under nineteen side. The other nominee was Alan Knott who naturally got selected. I did not.

In my final year at school, I had no fears of erratic treatment by the captain. I was the captain and was able to take seven wickets in one match and to take wickets against MCC Young Professionals and a Kent county side, which in those days was called Kent club and ground and which included players on the staff and good club players. I also had some good games for London Schools and played against a Somerset side that included Nick Rogers, a future friend at Oxford University. This successful season followed immediately after the traumatic death of my mum and the subsequent pressure of doing A levels two weeks later.

As with the previous summer, Mr Pope got me to complete an English Schools nomination form, this time coupled with Graham Johnson, an outstanding opening batsman and off spinner. I had higher hopes this time of being selected but to no avail. Slightly piqued I went to Lord's and saw a boy from Leicestershire who was a very devastating opening bowler in what might have been my position. So, that was fair enough except he was clearly throwing the ball, something that had probably not been highlighted on his nomination form.

Later, I was to be a selector for the English Schools Under nineteens and we used to go and watch regional and county matches to aid selection. In 1963 I fancy it was a paper selection and, in most circumstances, there was an unwitting quota of one per County. If that was the case there was not much chance of my being preferred one year to Alan Knott and then to Graham Johnson. I reckon Mr Pope was being kind.

My cricket development in the early 1960s was given a boost when I joined the Dartford Cricket club. From the age of 16 until we went to Kenya in 1969, I was a principal opening bowler in the first team. This was before League cricket but Dartford had a very good fixture list playing against good Kent clubs. One of these, Tunbridge Wells keep remarkable archived records on their website. Recently I saw a scorecard from 1962 where they had scored 212-8 dec, away to Dartford. They took 66 overs to get them and listed in the bowling analysis is

Roger Truelove 23 overs 10 maiden 38 runs 5 wickets

However, in the next few years, at university and at the beginning of my teaching career, my bowling gradually deteriorated, rusted, and fell into general disrepair. Or at least it did so in my head. I probably missed the winter practice, developed technical weaknesses that I did not know how to combat and lost confidence.

The decline was not instant and there were some good days. I remember eight wicket spells against Linden Park from Tunbridge Wells and also away to Romford and Gidea Park in Essex.

I have also seen another bit of encouragement online.

There was an extremely strong club called Beddington, all seemingly sporting Surrey 2nd eleven sweaters.

There is a short extract from their copious online history. It is the end of the 1964 season, so I am at Oxford.

'In a fixture at Hesketh Park (Dartford's ground and a sometime venue for county cricket) Dartford did well to hold a Beddington side. Against a Dartford attack led by Truelove, who took 5-59, the visiting batsmen were made to look very ordinary'.

That was, if I remember, apart from one player who made a hundred, and I suspect he might be the author of that passage.

Playing for this cricket club meant a great deal to me and in the end, it is the only club I played for where I was picked as a bowler.

In March 1969 Christine and I married and decided to go and teach in Kenya where I did not expect to play cricket.

But lo, there was a long tradition of cricket in Kenya and a strong community of Asian cricketers some of whom played first class cricket in England. On a shopping trip from Kijabe in the Rift Valley to Nairobi, I popped into the Impala club and subsequently went along to some nets and they selected me for their Sunday side. Not to bowl but as an upper order batsman. The matting wickets there disguised some of my batting shortcomings and I started to get good scores and by the third season I was captain of their Kenya League side.

When we returned to England, I took up playing as a club cricketer and continued to do so till the age of fifty-nine, scoring a century in my penultimate year for Bapchild against the Mote at Maidstone. As a batsman, I could never aspire to the quality of cricket that I would most have enjoyed but did enough to get some satisfaction out of playing.

The best times were playing for the Sittingbourne club Gore Court, then one of the stronger sides in the Kent League. I was lucky to play with my bank manager, Steve Tombs, a parsimonious seam bowler, and Keith Garrard, who I had bowled against as a young teenager for Dartford against Broadstairs, when Keith was much revered by my teammates, batting in his Incogniti cap. Keith was also a very good wicketkeeper and captain but quite strikingly, he was one of those rare cricketers who could not bowl at all.

Playing with Keith, I once opened the batting for the Gore Court second side at the very well-appointed Midland Bank ground in Beckenham. On ninety-six not out I hit the ball to deep square leg and decided to run for four. The only barrier to achieving that was if the fielder who had had to run round from mid-wicket could hit the leg stump directly from the boundary. He did! I was asked why I even took the risk and the truth is I had been fretting about our scoring rate and wanted to keep the strike. It was not the only time I was out on ninety-nine and once playing for a Reading side a good friend declared when I was not out ninety-seven. He was teaching me a lesson and I should have acknowledged that but it took a little time. I did score 100s on a few occasions.

What I also did for about twenty-five years, was to get deeply involved in the coaching and organisation of youth cricket. I organised cricket at club colt, school, district, county, regional and national level, consuming hours of precious time not only on attending matches and coaching courses, but also meetings all over the country on committee work. I ran the Kent Schools under nineteen side for many years, was a selector for the English Schools and was Treasurer of the English Schools for nine years.

I also organised coaching courses at different age groups within the south east region. One was for under thirteens at Dartford, where a very small boy called Nasser Hussain bowled well controlled leg breaks and a strong fast bowler called Alex Tudor arrived late because of a bomb scare at a London station. They are now media cricket personalities, as are other boys from that era.

I started my many years of managing Kent Schools sides in the mid-1970s. Managing meant eliciting nominations from schools, selecting sides, and making sure the boys reached the match venues, arranging umpires and scorers, checking lunch and tea arrangements and then on the match days, where we had no qualified coaches, providing the cricketing guidance on tactics, preparation, and individual techniques. Late in my career, I gave a promising batsman some advice on batting technique only for an irate dad to withdraw him from the side, because my advice had been interpreted as criticism. As time went on anxious fathers did try to intervene too much. In the worst cases, they had never played cricket themselves.

This illustrated a wider issue. There were always some boys who were very much better than their peers. If they were in England sides, high expectations were forced upon them, sometimes through local or even national newspapers. A wide range of people would invest vicarious commitment in their reputations, in schools, clubs, counties and regions of the country. The consequence, in my view, was that around some outstanding boys there was a nexus of supporters who preferred to hear only positive and laudatory comments about their proteges. A number proceeded into first class and even test cricket, had good careers, but may have been even better had more intervention been made in their development at the right time in their youth. For a period, I listened to coaches who could observe a flaw in a young player's technique but were reluctant to try to make amendments. These flaws were later tested at the highest level. I doubt whether this happened in Australia.

The 1970s are known as the Glory Years of Kent cricket with the county club winning nine trophies. This sense of Kentish superiority worked its way down the cricket pyramid. Club cricket in the recently created Kent League was of a very high standard, whilst the quality of our youth cricket persuaded us to believe that Kent's glory years had an assured future. It did not quite work out that way.

From those early days, I can now remember probably eight outstanding young cricketers in our Kent Schools sides. They all subsequently played first class cricket and three played in test cricket. What I think is interesting is that there is always a debate about the recruitment of young cricketers and the predominance of independent school boys in county and test cricket. It was also often asserted in the 1970s that cricket had died in the state schools. Yet of that 1970s elite, only Richard Ellison and Mark Benson attended independent schools, whilst Neil Taylor, Graham Dilley, Simon Hinks, Derek Aslett, Stuart Waterton, and Nigel Felton all went to state schools, and not just to Kent's grammar schools.

In truth, nobody was ever developed as an elite cricketer just by playing state school cricket. What worked then was that schools played enough to be able to pass on gifted youngsters to representative cricket and thence to county cricket clubs. Today, the crucial role must be played by clubs, who not only need to welcome keen and promising young players, both boys and girls, but to promote the game in their districts.

By the turn of the century, the business of schooling the best young cricketers passed from associations run by school teachers, to a much more professional structure, with qualified coaches tutoring sides in match situations. There is an obvious rationale for this and I supported it. However, as far as Kent is concerned, the contrast between those days of amateurish and enthusiastic school teacher activity and the modern professionalism with a dedicated academy, produces some interesting outcomes. In the 1980s, for example a Kent county championship side, excluding the overseas player, was made up almost exclusively of cricketers schooled in Kent and having played in our Kent schools' sides. It was a great joy recently when Kent won the 2022 one- day county competition, but only three of the side had been schooled in Kent youth cricket. After twenty or so years of an academy in Canterbury, I struggle to name any top-class bowler to be produced for the county side, apart from James Tredwell.

Clearly, I enjoyed doing all this but I regret it now for the time taken up was time I should have given to my wife and two older children, which I cannot give them back now. At a more selfish level, I should have been using this time and energy for my teaching career and latterly for my role in politics. I have little doubt that politics is more important than cricket and I wish I had got into it earlier.

In 1978, I put forward the enterprising idea that we could promote youth cricket, by publishing a magazine for and about young cricketers. The English Schools Cricket Association secretary, Cyril Cooper, and I made several visits to the home of Ben Brocklehurst the owner of the *Cricketer Magazine* near Tunbridge Wells where the entertainment was lavish and the willingness to embrace our venture enthusiastic. We produced a *Young Cricketer* magazine that included articles by Colin Cowdrey, Reg Simpson and Wilf Wooller and a lead report by one of our team that had just toured India, Derek Pringle. The hope was we would sell about 20,000 in the newsagents and 20,000 through the schools' associations. We reached the shop target and the schools sold practically none. We never repeated the initiative.

I did however join Ben and Belinda Brocklehurst for the final of the inter schools under 15 competition at Edgbaston, which was sponsored by the Lord's Taverners, sponsorship that Ben had lobbied for. On the strength of that Ben and Belinda felt entitled to lay on the most lavish catering arrangements, involving more fine wines and spirits than we would generally associate with an Under 15 cricket match. The school's association had booked us into a hotel which was quite pleasant but had to be abandoned as soon as it was clear that it was alcohol free.

I was used to their strong appetites but really could not believe it when on the train back to Euston Mrs Brocklehurst asked the ticket collector to arrange for some coffee.

Selecting the English Schools sides in the late 1970s and 1980s inevitably meant seeing some future England players in their developing years. At the time Mark Ramprakash, Graham Thorpe and Michael Atherton were regarded as the most likely boys to succeed at the highest level.

On one occasion we convened at a college in Liverpool for a game at the Aigburth cricket ground. Although only sixteen, Atherton was in the under nineteen side to bat and to bowl his leg breaks. When these teams were pulled together from across the country most boys were keen to fit in and be accepted by others. So, if a kick about football game was started, they all wanted to take part. But Atherton seemed to be a boy of singular self-possession and when I arrived, rather than the football and the team, he was making himself a pot of tea and engaging with the other selectors. In recent years he has been an eminent cricket correspondent for the *Times* and an authoritative commentator for Sky cricket.

Given that he played his Test career when every team in the world had at least one outstanding quick bowler, and often on unreliable wickets, his test record was outstanding and better than some with higher averages.

Another current media cricket heavy also appeared at one of our games. I regularly irritated my colleagues by arguing that the fixtures and grounds played on were not really commensurate with the idea that boys had earned the right to play as youth internationals.

We played Welsh Schools, which was somewhat akin to England playing a test match against Glamorgan. The games did not greatly add to the development of sometimes outstanding young cricketers.

We were taken to what was essentially a village pitch just outside Swansea and we had selected, on the basis of public school cricket, a fastish tall bowler from Uppingham School called Jonathan Agnew.

Like Atherton, he was good at chatting up the selectors, and before play started convinced the team manager that it would be better for him to bowl off spinners in the prevailing conditions on the ground.

He was allowed to do so. I thought that was a bit of a mockery and in the event, he was not remotely suited to off spin bowling.

In 1986, the English schools branched out into a new representative age group side, inviting Sri Lanka to send an under seventeen side here for a series of one day and three-day matches. I was appointed team manager and Les Lenham, a former Sussex batsman, the coach, at which he was highly regarded.

It was my idea to recruit Les. Before that, match management of these sides was reserved exclusively to English schools' members. This caused much debate, as county cricket clubs and the National Cricket Association, at that time, felt emerging players needed something more professional.

So, Les and I entered new territory and it had to be a learning experience. I retained responsibility for selection, which he may have found hard to accept, and he did all the in-match guidance, which I had always done with representative sides. The transition to a more professional set up continued and is how things are done today.

The first one day game at Uxbridge began badly. The two captains, both of whom became test cricketers, went out to toss. Coming back to our dressing room, John Crawley told our openers to pad up to bat. Unfortunately, Marvan Atapattu, the Sri Lankan captain, had gone back to his side and told his openers to do the same. They both claimed to have won the toss. In the confusion I said they must toss again, with the umpires this time being present. This was not a popular decision.

Sri Lanka won the second round of tossing and won the match comfortably. England won the next game at Chelmsford and the decider at the Oval was abandoned through rain. The three-day matches were both drawn. At Taunton, our not very fast bowlers pitched too short to test the Sri Lankan's out. They were very good at hooking and passed a score of 300 in the first innings. Apart from John Crawley, our side included two other future test players, Ronnie Irani and Aftab Habib and Sri Lanka had a bowler of medium pace cutters, called Kumar Dharmasena, who is one of the world's elite umpires.

Following, this relatively successful series, moves took place to make under seventeen cricket a key part of the youth development process. As I have indicated, there was a gradual transition from school associations running representative youth cricket towards more professional engagement.

On one occasion, I had to go to Oundle School to link up with various coaches to help run an under seventeen development festival. Several coaches at that time were ex professional cricketers and they really enjoyed repeating stories from their playing days,

On the first night, I settled down in bed next to a room heavily populated by coaches and a generous supply of whisky. The fun was largely orchestrated by David Lloyd and it went on loudly into the early hours.

At breakfast the next morning, David Lloyd courteously asked me whether I had had a good night.

No, was my curt reply.

I then rehearsed the many stories I had overheard through the early hours, one about a run up mix up by two county openers that had enjoyed an outing about every fifteen minutes for several hours.

Lloyd found this exceedingly funny.

On another occasion, we were selecting a side and choosing between two wicket keepers, one of whom, in my opinion, was very talented and the other very ordinary. There was amongst the coaches a surprising preference for the ordinary boy and this was backed up by an arch suggestion that the talented one was not a good learner, for obvious reasons, and those reasons I inferred from a very unpleasant expression was due to his race.

The better wicket keeper went on to have a good career as a professional cricketer, along with his equally talented brother.

So, whilst it was inevitable that outstanding schoolboy cricketers should receive technical tuition from high quality coaches, there were good pastoral and educational reasons why teachers should also be involved.

I stopped being an officer for the English Schools in 1992. There were too many other distractions by then.

I would have done it before but for my sense of loyalty to the secretary Cyril Cooper. It is never acknowledged that Cyril, after a lunch, he and I had had with Trevor Bailey, was responsible for the introduction of Kwik Cricket into this country.

Today, I watch a lot of cricket on television. I watch Kent occasionally but I have also returned to my primary school days by going to watch Surrey matches at the Oval. I like to walk right around the ground at times and reflect warmly on those early days when I developed such a consuming interest in what is only a game. What I most enjoy is going to a match with my sons, who are both shrewd and wise judges of the game, or with my nephew Simon or with friends like Derek Wyatt, Steve Telfer, Dick Calvert, and Tom Ledger.

Inevitably cricket has moved on from those happy days of the 1950s and 1960s. It is no longer just a season of three-day county cricket matches, broken by five test matches with tourists, who played serious fixtures with the counties.

Like most people of my age, I prefer 'proper' cricket but I can see that the shorter forms of the game have helped cricket to survive and to introduce new skills. However, our administrators have now got the balance wrong, and their motives do seem to be about short-term commercial interests rather than cricket.

To be precise, the Hundred is abhorrent, an unnecessary additional variant on the T20 games, having a disastrous impact on championship cricket and preparation for test cricket.

Trying to invent new affinities does not work especially if it is based on franchising.

For short term financial reward, the future of cricket is put at risk. There is too much influence from Sky, denying terrestrial viewers the best cricket, determining the fixture programme, and intruding too much into the games themselves. I have cricket loving friends who will not watch on Sky, because of an aversion to its ownership.

Sport has played a big part in my families. My brothers

were good at sport and very enthusiastic. Owen was a good rugger player, an athlete and not bad at cricket and golf either. Jim was a fine rugger player and even won a boxing medal in the RAF. My daughter Catherine was a promising athlete and should have had more encouragement and my wife Christine was also a keen runner in her teens and enjoys badminton. John and Richard both played cricket and when they scored runs, they did it elegantly. None, however, have ever been as obsessive or yearned so much for success, as I have about cricket. Of course, I am not alone.

It's only a game.

4

TEDDY HALL

For my south London working class family, for my modest south London school and for me, with transparent south London characteristics, entry to one of the world's most distinguished universities was a singular thing. Some of my teachers believed that my most obvious asset was a kind of adaptability, a capacity perhaps to catch on easily to a changed set of mores. Things rubbed off on me that have never really gone away, a slight change of speech patterns and a sense of having been privileged for no significant reason.

I have always felt lucky and that luck must have played some part in my winning entry.

I went up to Oxford in October 1963, to St Edmund Hall, known universally as Teddy Hall. I stayed a student at 'The Hall' until 1967, taking a history degree and then doing a diploma in education, to qualify to teach.

St Edmund of Abingdon was a thirteenth century academic called Edmund Rich who taught Aristotelean philosophy in Paris and Oxford where he established the Hall as a place of learning. He also became Archbishop of Canterbury in 1234.

To get there from the Oxford station, I had to walk

through Carfax and practically all the way down the High to Queen's College, then left into Queens Lane and just on the right is the modest entrance to the Hall. This leads into the front quad which is familiar to ITV viewers of the Morse derivative Lewis, as they seem to do a lot of filming there. To the left is the old dining hall and at the far end of the quad is an entrance to the back of the college which has been considerably developed since I was there. It is not one of the grand well-endowed colleges of Oxford like Christ Church, founded by Thomas Wolsey, or Trinity or Balliol. But in those days, it had a distinctive role within the University. It was a magnet for gifted sportsmen, within the college and across the University. In short, if you wanted to get noticed you hung around the Teddy Hall quad as much as possible. The bar, called the buttery, was also the place to be and on long evenings uninhibited and somewhat inebriated youths would join in serenading the lady custodian of the buttery, who was familiar to many as Mrs B. Mind you, by 1963, Mrs B had formed the view that the intake to the Hall, and the University in general, now contained too many undergraduates who were not gentlemen. Me, for example. This jaundiced view was shared by some of our tutors, one complaining that it was not the same trying to impart knowledge to young boys, who had not done National Service. Well, that was his excuse.

After I left Oxford, I heard that Mrs B left the Hall abruptly.

We had college servants, a privilege I really did not want. At that time the people of Oxford had the opportunity to earn good wages in the car factories in Cowley, whereas the college earnings were low. Some of our attendants reminded me of Dogberry and Verges in *Much Ado About Nothing.*

To confirm admission into the Hall we each individually had to recite a commitment in Latin, even those who had never studied Latin. So, I became an alumnus of Aula Sancti Edmundi along with all the other Aularians. I know I am not forgotten, because they kindly ring me up from time to time, to ask after my health and to offer me the opportunity to contribute to the university costs of today's students.

The presence of too many manifestly ungentlemanly youths at this time was part of a radical change in the country's approach to higher education. In 1963 the Government published the Robbins Report which proposed a major expansion of university education, new universities, and the conversion of colleges of advanced technology to university status. Crucially it called for all those of intellectual potential to be given the opportunity to study at this level. It was the UK catching up and nowhere in the report did it mention the need to be a gentleman.

A recent perceptive book by Simon Kuper, an undergraduate in the 1980s, suggests that the progressive change imagined in the 1960s did not materialise. His book is about how a small group of public school, privileged and entitled young Conservatives developed their political skills in the Oxford Union and in the University Conservative Association and now dominate our politics in the 2020s. This includes Cameron, Osborne, Johnson, Gove, and Rees Mogg, but also members of the elite political media such as Nick Robinson. Self-regarding and presumptuous, they regarded Oxford as an inevitable stepping stone to power. Debating in the Oxford Union was about skills not principles, how to play the game and Kuper suggests that has carried over into their political lives in our time.

Thatcherism and the beginnings of Brexitism were the prevailing zeitgeist of their time in Oxford, in contrast to the 1960s when there was a veneer of progressivism, not actually shared by all.

Oxford graduates dominate not only in the Conservative party and media, but right across our public services with people like Simon Stevens in the health service. Many of the questionable contracts during the Covid pandemic went to Oxford chums. And, of course, Oxford is prominent in leading parts of the Labour Party. The Milibands, Ed Balls and Yvette Cooper were all at Oxford, and Keir Starmer took a second degree in Teddy Hall, after first graduating at Leeds. But the path to leadership in the Labour Party is not as assured and inevitable as it has become in the Conservative Party. Even so, as Kuper pointed out, eleven of our fifteen post war Prime Ministers, both Conservative and Labour were Oxonians, the four exceptions being Churchill, Callaghan, Major and Brown. Since Kuper's book was published two more Oxonians have held the highest office, Liz Truss from Merton, and Rishi Sunak from Lincoln.

Kuper also focusses on the discomfort that some students from state school backgrounds felt in an alien social environment. I do not think I felt that in the 1960s. I felt

I belonged and where I found that social elitism and privilege existed, I spoke against it, but that was just part of my persona. I suspect I had the Oxonian tendency to argue a case strongly and with conviction even if with very limited knowledge. The insecurities I felt at the time were more to do with a sense of having no home base with the death of my mum and uncertainty about how I would live after university.

Perhaps it was that perceived adaptability.

Supporting the Labour Party, and after 1964 supporting that 'horrible little man, Wilson' was in the opinion of some of my colleagues a singularly unmannered thing to do, and was more appropriate to redbrick universities. That was the Harold Wilson who took an applauded first from Jesus College by the way.

There was a strong Oxford University Labour Club and for many reasons I regret only going to a few of their meetings. I did try some more extreme left groups and shared with Harold Wilson a lack of empathy with the public school Marxists there. Where I had come from, there were not many who were fixated on whether Trotsky or Stalin were the true prophets of socialism.

Thus, the political climate meant that by 1963 both Oxford and Cambridge felt the pressure to recruit from a wider range of schools and to overcome a sense of social exclusivity. What was the social ambience in 1963?

There is an amusing poem by D.H. Lawrence called *The Oxford Voice*. Written in 1928, a different time but worthy of reflection.

Lawrence prodded away against something that sought

to be

"...so seductively superior, so seductively

Self effacingly

Deprecatingly

Superior,

We wouldn't insist on it for a moment

But we are

You admit it we are

Superior."

Lawrence also targeted the *Would Be Oxford Voice,* those in search of a magic social veneer that would help them through a difficult life.

This is not simply about affecting a superior accent; it is about adopting a confident distinctive air, based not on natural qualities but merely on an assumption of superiority. Was it still part of Oxford in 1963? Yes, it was.

I had heard all about Oxford's unique one-to-one tutorial system. In fact, in our college, it was not one-to-one but one-to-two. Each of us was required to read out our weekly essays and that plus a few desultory introductory comments and the setting of more essays for the following week, effectively exhausted the allocated hour without any actual teaching taking place. The essays were never assessed. They simply passed a soporific afternoon. Book lists were issued but without much advice as to where to start and where to end.

It was a fairly unique misuse of public money. As far as we could see the same essays were set every year, and the students in the year above were helpful. Seminars and lectures outside the Hall were of much more use. I am absolutely sure that teaching in St Edmund Hall is far better now. Much more is expected both of students and tutors, whilst Oxford's attempts to recruit from a wider talent pool, through contextual admissions that factor in the challenges to learning that young people have made, has caused anxiety not least from the government, less Etonians and others might lose their traditional advantage.

Though the essays were never assessed even verbally, we did briefly receive some feedback during the first term, preparing for the 'Prelims,' which were the only formal examinations before Finals at the end of the third year. For 'Prelims' we did some historical geography and had to study and translate one French text, L'ancien Regime et La Revolution by de Tocqueville and one in Latin, Historia ecclesiastica gentis Anglorum by the Venerable Bede.

When we got back our practice translations, they were corrected and awarded a grade. I think the first one I did receive a VS+.

The grading was in Latin, and not in Roman numerals, but in three descriptive and essentially grudging terms. They were Satis=Alright; Vix Satis=scarcely acceptable; and Non Satis=do it again. As ever, inventive variations were built around these basic alternatives so that VS+ was just above scarcely acceptable and the next stage up would be VS+/S-, a state of grace somewhere between the best scarcely acceptable and the weakest attempt at being satisfactory. None of the twelve historians in my group seemed especially good at languages but we all passed first time at Christmas.

One afternoon in late November 1963, I was in a small study at the end of our Junior Common Room doing a bit of prep for the Prelim exams when somebody said there was a rumour that something appalling had happened in Dallas Texas. I got up and walked through the common room and through one conversation after another it became more and more evident that the American President John F Kennedy had been shot and a few hours later it was reported that he had died. I heard someone say that that would lead to Johnson becoming President, apparently 'a Southern Democrat of the very worst kind.'

It was a signal moment for us all at that time. Sadly, other assassinations followed through the 1960s, all of the victims on the left of the American political spectrum. The fact that so many Americans support the NRA gun lobby in the USA and equate owning a gun with liberty always makes me wonder whether we really are in the same cultural place.

It was not quite true to say that we never had any serious or professional teaching in the Hall. For the modern European history papers, they brought in some outside help in the form of J.P.D Dunbabin, who later became a college don. He organised effective seminars and gave very critical responses to any shoddy work. Dunbabin became a major authority on modern international relations and in 2017 was presented with a 'Lifetime Achievement Award' by All Party Parliamentary historians, the presentation being made by Nick Thomas Symonds, the then shadow Home Secretary and an Aularian.

I did not start well with Dunbabin. Reprising the Mr Bean moments of my interview week, one Saturday morning it was my turn to present to a seminar group a paper on Russian Foreign Policy prior to the First World War.

I caught the bus in from Iffley and running tight for time, I leapt off the bus at the stop opposite to Queens Lane and in landing ripped my trousers asunder. Knowing I would now be definitely late, I ran up the High to Shepherd and Woodward's, pushing back on the usual obsequious sales blandishments, bought some trousers and got to the seminar about 20 minutes late.

Bouncing into the room with a 'sorry I'm late I've been to buy trousers' did not set the right sort of tone and our tutor was clearly irritated, because he took his teaching role seriously.

As Stephen Hawking once said the prevailing feeling in Oxford was a pretence of not taking studies seriously. Students who did that were 'grey men.' The important thing was to be a 'nice chap' and frequently conversations about an individual were rounded off with the expected endorsement, 'of course he's a very nice chap.'

In my first week at Teddy Hall, I got picked for the Hall football team. I was given a fixture card for the whole winter season with a number of college fixtures bracketed with the word (Cantab.). Although I had done

Latin A level, it took me a few moments to realise that this indicated a fixture with a Cambridge College, of which there were several.

On the first Saturday morning, we travelled over from Oxford to Cambridge, stopping en route at Bedford and being well entertained for lunch when we got to Cambridge. On the way, there was a lot of interest in the day's football fixtures. Unsurprisingly I was the only Charlton supporter on board.

The voices on the coach were not the 'Oxford Voice.' Only one of the team was from an independent school and the majority were from either Yorkshire or Lancashire grammar schools. The pitch we played on was excellent and we won well. I was asked to play at outside right, in the old W formation, and although I had never done that before, I linked up well with the inside right, Brian Hardcastle from Huddersfield, who was also the captain of the full University side. Though I never got into that side, football at Oxford gave me more opportunities than my favoured sport, cricket, and at the time, I thought that that reflected the different social backgrounds associated with the sports. Apart from enjoying playing for the Hall first team, I played quite a lot for the Oxford University Centaurs, playing representative matches against public schools, London University Colleges and on one occasion Sandhurst Army College.

One Saturday, I had a purple patch playing for the Centaurs against St Mary's College in Twickenham, winning the game with two spectacular long-range shots, with either foot. The following Saturday, we played the

Sandhurst match at Iffley Road. Probably of no significance, but I spent the previous day in London with a French girl-friend. Early in the Sandhurst match I broke through the middle, ran from the halfway line, and then shot past the goalkeeper, just inside the post. The corner post! Bad start that just got worse and worse.

On another occasion I played for the Centaurs at Bradfield College, near Pangbourne. For some reason the match was reported in the Guardian newspaper. My former teachers were pleased to see Truelove (Addey and Stanhope and St Edmund Hall) in the published team list and the fact I scored one of our seven goals.

On that first Saturday in Cambridge, I discovered that it was intended to be a long day. After the match we had tea, listening intently to the football scores. Charlton incidentally won away at Northampton that day, I really do remember such worthless things. It was October 19, 1963 and they won two-one, goals by Kenning and Matthews.

The evening was then spent in a Cambridge pub.

The coach drivers accepted this, with some pecuniary encouragement and it was generally the case that we got back to Oxford after midnight and after the closure of the college gates.

One of the students had a bedroom that backed on to the High. Whoever got assigned that room knew that he would never have any peace on a Saturday night, not only from fairly well sauced footballers but from any party goer who had been out for the night. The occupant inevitably became the host for all night parties and those that attended them, as I did, phlegmatically adjusted to the constant banging on the window and the climbing in and passage through of an eclectic cross section of the Hall population, and possibly guests.

The football team included two other freshmen whose friendship and support I valued throughout my time in Oxford. Neither of them bought into the Oxford Voice or being a Hall Man imperative. They were both very self-possessed as they were.

One was Nick Rogers, who played right half and the other John Haines who played on the left wing. As John and I were both from London, we were regarded as a bit fancy dan and best used on the wings.

I had met Nick in August. He was playing for Somerset young cricketers and I was playing for London schools. He came from a grammar School in Bruton in Somerset. He was also related to the famous Graveney cricketing family from Gloucestershire. In College, we were required to wear gowns to tutorials and for evening meals. The majority of us were regarded as 'commoners' and required to wear short gowns, whilst a small number had been awarded scholarships and exhibitions and wore gowns, the length of which signalled a kind of academic superiority. Of the twelve history undergraduates in my year, two wore long gowns. That did not include either Nick or me. Yet, in my view, he was by some distance the best historian amongst us. Undergraduate students are not by definition historians; nor are conscientious school teachers sharing their knowledge as best they can with their classes. Historians are individuals with a self-disciplined passion for research, detail and accuracy based on critical analyses of sources. They add to the sum of our knowledge and throw light on new places and new issues. They are rigorously committed to evidence rather than speculation and vague theorising. I am not a historian. Nick Rogers is.

He became history professor at the York University in Toronto, is an acknowledged expert on eighteenth century British history, is widely published and his retirement was celebrated by an International Conference. On a recent Lecture tour to Bristol, he took time out to show Christine and me round his home city whose local history he knows so well.

John Haines read what was known in Oxford as Jurisprudence, in other words Law. He said it was tedious, simply soaking up law and past cases, no opportunity to theorise or speculate about ideas. He has had a successful career as a barrister. He could not be an Oxford Voice or Hall man because already written into his DNA was North London Man. That was in the mid-1960s and North London man was a fashionable, trendy thing to be and as I was informed by John and his many North London friends a very different thing to a South London man, of which I was of course a pitiable example. I have not seen much of John since University, apart from sharing a match at Highbury with Arsenal just beating Charlton two-one.

My years at Oxford were not a time of great stability and security. The loss of my mum was traumatic both in fact and manner. Apart from my thoughtful aunt, my mum's sister, looking after our house, there was no home to go to, with the rest of my family scattered around.

Sometimes I stayed in Oxford during vacations, one year I used the summer to go to South America as a distinctly unworthy Merchant seaman (DHU-Deck Hand Unqualified). Sometimes I stayed with my brothers and their understanding wives.

One summer I did a hitchhiking tour of part of the north of England, visiting Jim and Carole in Louth, where he was stationed. I then went on to Huddersfield to visit a good friend from the year above called Richard Taylor. His father was headmaster of the grammar school in Almondbury and I discussed with Mr Taylor the desirability or otherwise of a closer relationship between the Labour and Liberal Parties. We also visited the school that Harold Wilson had attended and we went down into the valley to visit Brian Hardcastle and his family. Richard had a nice sister who once accompanied me at a Teddy Hall summer ball.

I was always anxious to get back to Oxford.

I used to like simply walking around the city and still do: for example, from Teddy Hall, cross over to Merton Street, down past Corpus Christi and down to Christ Church; go through the Meadow and then to Magdalen College Bridge, along the river and up to the Parks, round to St Giles where Latimer and Ridley lit a light throughout Europe; left past Trinity and then past the Ashmolean and Bodleian, to the High and back down to the Hall.

There was a lot of cinema going; for example, up to Headington for *Goldfinger*,

'Do you expect me to talk?'

'No Mr Bond I expect you to die'

Also, to Headington to see *Butterfield 8*, so appalling we walked out after half an hour

Much better was an evening in Walton Street to see for the first of many times Hitchcock's masterpiece of 1938 the *Lady Vanishes*, the only time I have seen a packed cinema audience rise at the end in universal and spontaneous applause. There was also a special showing of *Lawrence of Arabia*, with a military band and an introduction by the mayor, who forgot the name of the Band Leader. There was a special cheer when Lawrence, played by Peter O'Toole, is asked whether Oxfordshire is a desert country.

'No, a fat country; fat people'

'You are not fat'

'No, I am different'

However, the most talked about film of that time was called *The Servant*. It was written by Harold Pinter and directed by Joseph Losey. It starred Dirk Bogarde, James Fox, and Sarah Miles, and it was sinister, erotic, and apparently full of hidden symbolism such as dripping taps and staircase banisters that looked like a prison. It was backed by appropriately dark moody music from John Dankworth. It is about a servant taking psychological control of his aristocratic employer by ruthlessly exploiting his desires and shortcomings. It was obviously about class. It seemed to have something to say to an Oxford audience during what was supposed to be a social change in the university. There was much in it to talk about and a lot of the discussion was monumentally pretentious. It was very sixties, if that means anything. It was very Harold Pinter, the author of the equally sinister *Birthday Party*.

We also went to the theatre, to the Oxford Union and to pubs in and around Oxford.

Of course, I played cricket. Having had a good season before going to Oxford, I thought I might be considered for the University side whose fixtures then were still regarded as first class, though that was already an anachronism. I was not considered. I learned after a while that serious thought was only given to freshmen who had done particularly well in public school cricket or to state schoolboys who had played for county cricket sides, either first or second elevens, or for the English Schools. So, I was near, but not near enough. I am too inclined to be self-effacing and then when frustrated volatile and angry. Neither works. I might have done better to have gone to Kent the previous year and asked for a couple of games in their Second team. After all, I had worked hard in their development nets for seven years. They could only have said no. And as I played football with the University cricket captain throughout the winter, I might have had the chutzpah to have at least mentioned how near I had got to the English Schools side. I did none of that and as I said in the previous chapter my cricket went into decline.

One day when changing for football at Iffley Road, I saw an alternative example of live opportunism. Nearby was a group of athletes getting changed with one quite small man with a large voice and an obvious propensity for dominating conversation, boasting, it seemed to me, about how involvement in Oxfam could secure him advantageous connections. I did not much like the look of this little man but did not know his name. I was told he was called Jeffrey Archer. He was in Oxford to do a diploma in education. He was not in Oxford for academic reasons but he had apparently attracted the Beatles to some event. Successful as he may have been at self-promotion, I would not wish to emulate him in any way.

I took finals in 1966, but not before going home for a couple of days during the general election, to help the Labour Party in my home constituency, of Woolwich East. For the first time I knocked on doors and went back to a committee room with returns from my canvassing. I thought the whole process was fascinating, all that working out the turnout and our share of it.

Our share was in fact seventy-one per cent across the constituency and Labour had a majority over the Conservatives of 111 seats. In all truth, it was one of the rare occasions that Labour has won with a clear majority.

Christopher Mayhew won again in Woolwich, as he did eight times, before joining the Liberal Party after 1974.

Later in the summer of 1966, I was at home, of course, for the World Football Cup final. We went over to my uncle Bert's at Eltham and on the Sunday, I went to the cinema in London where the whole audience stood and cheered when the Pathe News showed highlights from the day before. It was one of those moments when it is hard not to cry; somewhat like the Thursday night street clapping that we did for our frontline workers in the Covid 19 crisis.

After graduating in 1966, I went back to Oxford to do a diploma in education, as I had always wanted to teach. I thought that I might try to diversify my sporting activities a little and signed up for horse riding lessons. There was a girl there showing us what to do and in a slightly strange kind of way I liked her. However, she told me she preferred horses to people and being the wrong sort of species, I gave up on riding, principally because I was so bad at it. I was not much better at hockey or rugby union and I have to confess I cannot understand how any rational or feeling human being would prefer playing those games rather than football.

Then, I was offered the most extraordinary opportunity. Instead of doing the teaching practice in England, an inevitable part of doing an education diploma, I was sent instead to the Phillips Academy in Exeter, New Hampshire, for a term from January to April 1967.

It was an eccentric idea. The host school paid my fare to the United States and our Government enhanced my usual student grant. It was normal for teaching practices to be evaluated by an education department tutor but that was clearly impractical. I was allowed to self-assess.

The Phillips Academy is in a small town called Exeter about sixty miles north of Boston. It was not an ordinary school. It was probably the most academically successful school in the United States and sent most of its graduate students to the top Ivy League universities and predominantly to Harvard. It was one of a group of Prep schools, not preparatory as they are in England, but to prepare students for the highest levels of university education. Many of the students had astronomically high

IQs. Its many prosperous students and alumni funded scholarships for outstanding boys (it was boys then, it is co-ed now) from poorer backgrounds, and especially from black communities. The intake was from all over the United States and the school used alumni to scout around for boys of remarkable intellectual potential. I have taught in schools with a different intake.

The teaching I did was more like conducting a university seminar. The classes were set reading tasks from distinctly scholarly text books. There were only about twelve in a class and my role, which I practiced under supervision, was to prompt discussion around issues that arose from the reading. I taught, or rather tutored, a class in Russian history, because they genuinely wanted to understand Russia better and we also did classes in Marxism without any thoughts of McCarthyism.

My colleagues were very cerebral.

With one exception. I was given half of a fine bungalow to live in and in the other half was a PE teacher and his wife. One evening they popped in for a chat about the world and his view of the world was not very close to mine or to the other liberal minded people in Exeter.

Annexed to some rather extreme conservative views was his conviction that Hitler was still alive, that he was in South America plotting the overthrow of the corrupt United States government, that Hitler had been responsible for the lights going out in Massachusetts in 1965 and in summary, the sooner he came and sorted out America the better.

I cannot exaggerate how much I enjoyed being at Exeter.

I had a friend at Harvard and went down to Boston regularly and watched ice hockey on a Saturday night. Phillips also organised opportunities to visit other schools to get a broader idea of American High School education. I went to one school in Boston, which seemed to have the same progressive liberal views as Phillips, only to be invited into the principal's office for a tirade about the way liberals were undermining American values and that a day of reckoning would come. This was 1967 and already he was predicting the rise of a conservative messiah from the west coast who would face down the communists and free the American people from the yoke of Federal Government. This messianic figure had just become Governor of California, had been a B movie actor and his name was Ronald Reagan.

I understand absolutely why the United States is such an ideologically divided country, able to go from Obama to Trump, from the sublime to the ridiculous.

I would gladly have returned to Exeter or somewhere similar but I soon found out that I would need an immigration visa and the implication of that was that if my number came up, I could be drafted into the war in Vietnam. Whilst I was there, I heard of a young French man who had arrived in America, been immediately drafted, and then just as swiftly killed. I did not actually think at the time that they should have been in Vietnam but when I offered this view to a good friend called Bernie Bradstreet in Harvard, I got a briefing on the domino theory and containment. I thought too many Americans had a one-dimensional view of communism in the world. The undergraduates at Harvard were required to read a text by Hans Morgenthau published in

1948 on the *Struggle for Power and Peace* which claims to be realistic about world power politics but propagated the view that American influence had to expand to hold back the spread of communism. Consequently, they went into conflict in places like Korea and Indo China, where possibly little immediate American interest was at stake.

Meanwhile in 1967 a British delegation was visiting General Dynamics in Fort Worth Texas, intending to commission the F111 supersonic fighter bomber, to meet the needs of British defence as we withdrew from East of Suez.

My brother Owen was there on behalf of the RAF and it was agreed that I would call on him and his wife Jennie.

I caught one of the famous Greyhound buses. You could buy a ninety-nine day ticket for ninety-nine dollars and travel anywhere across the United States. I picked up a bus from New York on a Saturday evening and arrived in Dallas on a Wednesday afternoon, before getting the onward bus to Fort Worth. En route we had gone through Pittsburgh, Cincinnati, and St. Louis and apart from the occasional bus stops I sat in the same seat for three and a half days. Some other passengers were going all the way to the West Coast. That was about a week's travelling.

After Oxford, I taught history at a boys' grammar school in Bromley. I lived with my now retired dad in his flat in Plumstead and we got on very well. We frequently went down the club, drunk quite a lot, got fish and chips on the way home, and talked a lot about Kent cricket.

For the next two summers he used to come and watch me play cricket at Dartford. He bought me a Hillman Imp which I drove to school but which also got us around to several cricket grounds. I do not think he had had that kind of matey relationship before.

For a time, I had a girl friend called Audrey. Unfortunately, when I went to her house, I had to listen to her father's endless diatribes against the Labour government plus a lot of dog hairs all over their furniture. But it was her mother who was the actual politician. I liked her and could not resist her invitation to attend her election count at the Woolwich Town Hall in May. The trouble was she was a Conservative and if I went, I could not help meeting some Labour Councillors I knew who would inevitably think I was there to support them.

The Town Hall was a fine building and the count was in the auditorium where I had performed in a gang show and where I had attended the Suez meeting in 1956. The Council provided two reception rooms for the Labour and Conservative parties to entertain their guests and supporters. I was expected to join Audrey and mum in the Conservative room.

But I had been spotted by Labour Councillor Dicky Neave and he ushered me into the Labour reception room where I nodded obediently as they rehearsed their contempt for the Conservative Party.

Eventually I managed to withdraw and found Audrey who wanted to know where I had been, naturally. We then went to the Conservative reception, where I heard this time about the catastrophic impact of Labour rule in Woolwich, the waste, and the rate levies.

After a while I whispered a desperate plea that we should

leave.

'Oh yes please, I don't like politics.'

Then in the summer of 1968, I was playing a game of cricket against a team called Blackheath Wanderers when rain stopped play. Having showered and changed I saw a very pretty girl sitting with her parents. I kept trying to find a way to introduce myself but took the coward's path and joined the others at the bar.

A little later, in September, I went to a party in Bromley and saw the same girl and this time summoned up the courage to talk and we started to see each other. I arranged to collect her one Sunday afternoon but as I journeyed from Plumstead to Crofton Park I was held up by flooding in Lewisham. I rang Christine and then detoured to Blackheath, New Cross, and Brockley.

Soon after that my cousin John Underdown got married and the reception was in Eltham. All our family were there and I was best man. By early evening I was missing seeing Christine and asked Jim to drive over to Crofton Park and ask her to come along for the rest of the evening. She did. We all had a good time, rounded off by dad making a dignified and courteous speech thanking the band for entertaining us all evening. We went back to dad's flat and I asked Christine how she responded to my dad thanking the band, when there was not any band present. She was fine.

On another occasion I had taken pupils from school to London and had to drive back from Bromley as the fog came down. As I approached Sydenham Hill from Southend Lane, I was gratified to see traffic from my left allowing me to come out to turn right. As I did so, I heard a strange sound on the bonnet of the car. It was a policeman who had been conducting traffic until I drove into him. Subsequently my insurance had to pay out for the pain he had suffered though at the time he was perfectly amenable.

'It's funny mate. I was on duty last weekend dealing with all those protesters outside Rhodesia House and I get away without a scratch. And now, all I'm doing is bit of traffic duty and some geezer goes and drives straight into me.'

I had to wait a while at the scene and a whole cavalcade of cars turned up to defend the police victim of unprovoked violence.

I wanted to see Christine as often as possible. She came to watch me play football and I said I would watch her play badminton. She thought that was very indulgent of me but I really enjoyed watching her play, much more interested in her movements than the movements of the shuttlecock.

Christine Lovell was teaching French at a Comprehensive School in Catford, called Sedgehill. She is an outstanding teacher. She had been to Kenya the year before. I said I wanted to do some teaching in Africa and asked optimistically whether she would come with me if I applied for the following year. She said she would. I asked if it would be okay if we married. She said it would. We went to Oxford for a weekend and stayed in Jericho and went to the theatre. Just about two months after meeting we told people we were engaged. We married in March, lived in dad's flat through the summer and left for Kijabe in the Central Province Kenya in September.

People who know us are aware of how close Christine and I are, but she does not like over expressive displays of love in public. I have been lucky to share life with a partner who I have always found very attractive and also someone who is a very good and kind person. I am proud of our children, for their intelligence and accomplishments but also, like their mother, for their decency and clear moral beliefs and behaviour.

From the age of eleven when my brothers left home to twenty four, I had got along all right. I had had a great time playing cricket and had had the unexpected privilege of being an Oxford student. But there was always a sense of insecurity there and a feeling of being ungrounded emotionally. My mum's premature death had added to that.

From the moment I married Christine on the 29 March 1969, that feeling went. I have been very lucky and fortunate too to have had such likeable and intelligent children.

5

IN AND OUT OF AFRICA

In my introductory chapter I claimed that having considered the prospect of early morbidity, other challenges in life can become less likely to induce anxiety. I still find this to be true but with one exception. I have become increasingly likely to imagine all kinds of mishaps from making journeys, sometimes as straightforward as driving from home to Brighton.

It was so different in 1969. The fact that Kenya had just had a high profile political assassination; that there were whispers of a revival of Mau Mau type activity in the Kiambu District we are aiming to go to and the fact that my wife was already expecting our first child, none of this could then deter us from our determination to work in Africa.

During our time there, we had close encounters with wide animals; camping in an inadequate tent in Tsavo and in Uganda; surrounded by a herd of elephants in Samburu; boating in a search for crocodiles on the lower reaches of the Nile; journeying to the birth of our daughter Catherine on a muddy road, rumoured to be visited by a leopard.

We chose the week that Idi Amin seized power from

Milton Obote to visit Kampala in Uganda. We breathed a sigh of relief when we crossed the border into Kenya, having seen far too many guns by roadsides on the journey back.

And there were other potentially unnerving events, like nearly dying from peritonitis, or being asked to risk the wrath of a whole village by turning up without exam papers.

All this we took in our stride at the age of twenty-five.

In September, we made the fourteen-hour journey to Nairobi Airport. There we were met by Pat and Bernard Crix, an affable and open couple from the African Inland Mission station at Kijabe, where I was due to teach. They took us into the city, to the New Stanley Hotel for lunch and gave us some background to life on the Kijabe School compound.

It was first and foremost a mission station. Apart from the school there was a Mission Hospital and this was largely run by Americans, whilst the school staff was made up of American, English, and African teachers. The headmaster was, I thought, a missionary running a school rather than a headmaster with a Christian mission.

He was keen to draw us all into a strong Christian community.

The students were all Kikuyus and the station was right in the middle of where recruitment had taken place of Mau Mau insurgents in the 1950s.

My teaching job was to prepare students who had passed a selective examination into Secondary Education, for O levels, set by the Cambridge University examinations board. I had to teach a mixture of African and British history, focussing in part on the British Constitution.

To get to Kijabe, we had to drive from Nairobi on the Nakuru road until we started to go down the eastern side of the Great Rift Valley. Then after passing an Italian Church, we turned off on to a marram road that cut through woodland for five miles before we got to Kijabe.

The name Kijabe is said to be 'place of winds' in Maasai. It was perched on the side of the Rift Valley and we were given the bungalow at the bottom of the compound. So, our view from the front of our new home was right down and across this spectacular physical feature.

All our private property was due to arrive by ship at a later and unknown date and so our new friends joined together to give us enough to settle in.

It was not long before there was an urgent knocking at the back of our bungalow. Opening our backdoor we were confronted by three women who seemed to have come to shout at us. We had no idea what they were saying and why they were apparently so offensive. In fact, they were only asking us if we wanted to buy some vegetables but they were doing it in the Kikuyu language, which does not have a mellow tone.

An elderly man called Hezekiah came down and explained to us the best way of trading with these ladies and also directed us up the hill to the village to buy some milk. This we did, and then as strongly advised in our induction course in London, we boiled it thoroughly. It was not that pleasant to drink.

Most of our shopping was done once a week in Nairobi. The timetable was worked out so that each of us had an afternoon off and until we bought a car, the Crixes took us in and let us explore.

The main shopping was done at a supermarket, called to avoid any confusion, the Supermarket. It was disturbing to see so many victims of polio outside having to beg for survival. After shopping we would go for lunch, sometimes at the Hilton, sometimes at the New Stanley, and we also went into the Indian part of the city and for the first time ate samosa. Kenya had a significant Indian population. Their families had been in Kenya from the days of the East African Protectorate before the first world war, enticed there by the British Colonial Office to be the shopkeepers and traders needed to meet the needs of the white settler farmers from upcountry.

I had had a passing interest in the history and politics of Kenya for some time. I was familiar with the names of Jomo Kenyatta, Tom Mboya and Jaramoji Oginga Odinga. I knew about its extensive ethnic and tribal diversity, had followed its first post- colonial general election in 1963, when the KANU party defeated and then absorbed the opposition KADU party into a one-party democracy.

In the immediate post-colonial era, it was impossible to establish a democracy on the Westminster model because all that would do is create hegemony for the largest tribes. Instead by 1969 Kenya had a single ruling party, but held strongly contested primary elections in which strong differences of an ideological kind could emerge between different candidates.

Tom Mboya, a Luo, was a charismatic figure, who rightly believed that Kenya needed to invest heavily in education in order to become a strong modern and inclusive economy. When we arrived, the country had universal primary or elementary education and then state secondary schools based on selection in most tribal areas, the exceptions being with the more nomadic tribal areas, such as the Maasai, where the will to be modernised was strongly resisted. In Nairobi and in the village of Kikuyu, there were elite national schools for the very brightest young people. There were emerging universities and teacher training colleges in many parts of the country. As it was not yet possible to provide universal secondary schooling, Kenyatta had told the people to set up their own self-help village schools, which they did and many rural villages had these schools, which followed the harambee tradition of self-help.

Two months before we arrived in Kijabe, Tom Mboya was assassinated. There were fears of growing unrest and it was felt that Kijabe was itself a sensitive place, with concerns for Americans who had previously been in the Congo.

This was explained to us before we left England in September 1969. We still decided to go and whilst we were there, we took comfort from our colleagues and from the apparent tranquillity in the village.

The compact in KANU between the two main tribes, the Kikuyu from Central Province, and the Luo from the West Province, was being undermined by Oginga Odinga's break away KPU party, but Mboya was not part of that.

To get around the country we needed a car and an American on the mission station arranged for us to buy a VW Beetle, slightly less than cost price because it was a demonstrator model. At the end of the first term, we set out for Mombasa on the coast with our inadequate tent and inadequate camping skills.

'You can't go wrong with a Beetle' the American said. That was reassuring as my awareness of car mechanics then and now was extremely poor.

We set out on the 300-mile journey but not far short of Hunter's Lodge, less than a third of the way, some kind of cable broke and we were stranded. We sort of pitched a tent on some hard ground near the road. Christine was now six months pregnant and could not do any lifting but she had a much better idea of how we might make the silly little tent habitable for the night. The next day we were towed to Tsavo and then were picked up by a friendly guy who took us to the coast and insisted on us sharing his excellent beach house for the following week. We were well fed, had exclusive access to the incredible beach and, as was the norm in Kenya for wazungus (Europeans) played bridge every night. Subsequently, we went to the coast a number of times, to Mombasa and Malindi, during our stay in Kenya, once taking the overnight eight-hour train from Nairobi to Mombasa.

We also travelled to Serengeti and Samburu. In Samburu we slept in an open hut with a herd of elephants outside. Our second Christmas there we crossed into Uganda and stayed in Kampala. Right in the middle of a coup by Idi Amin! We still managed to see Murchison Falls. We did camp out at one site where lions were said to be about and where I had to continually go outside the tent at night due to a virulent bout of diarrhoea.

During the first term at Kijabe, we went several times to the fresh water lake at Naivasha for tea, where George and Joy Adamson once raised an orphaned lion cub called Elsa, featured in a film called *Born Free*. We also went further up the road to the soda lake at Nakuru, famous for the stunning sight of thousands of flamingos.

One warm Saturday, we were confined to base to be part of the school speech day. It was hot and we had to sit in a clearing with a large assembly of proud parents and families who had walked miles across the extensive Kikuyu lands for the occasion. We sat there for six hours. We had a garrulous chair of governors but the longevity of the afternoon was due mostly to the fact that every verbose utterance was delivered in three languages; Kikuyu, Swahili, and English. It meant, of course, that cumulatively we listened to four hours of speech that we did not understand. Added to that, the Chair did not always choose his words wisely when speaking in English and might have been advised not to refer to the English and American wives as cows even if his intention, whatever it was, was innocent of any insult. There was quite a lot of discussion about this aberration during the evening.

At the end of the first term, the Government Education Ministry decided that I should be moved to Kikuyu a town nearer to Nairobi, to the Alliance Girls High School, so that I could teach A level History in addition to the O levels I had been doing in Kijabe. The two Alliance schools at Kikuyu, one for boys and the other girls, were the country's elite National schools. Just as the Phillips Academy in the United States had scoured the country for the brightest youngsters, so the Government in Kenya went all over to find the most able girls to come to Kikuyu.

They had even persuaded the Maasai to allow a couple of girls to join us and they were effectively pioneering.

So, apart from visiting friends, and going to the hospital for the birth of Catherine, our time in the extraordinary Kijabe setting was over. It is interesting to see it is now a small town, with a railway station on the route from Nairobi to Nakuru, and that the hospital is still an important service to the local community.

The boys' school at Kikuyu had been opened in 1926 and the girls in 1948. They had both been founded by Protestant missions.

There were three striking contrasts with Kijabe, further up country. Whilst there were still many girls from rural villages, where the economics of life were still basically subsistent, there were also many from rich families in Nairobi, daughters of government ministers or of emerging commercial and finance driven classes. Most African students at this time were generally conscientious but passive learners, unlikely to challenge or question what they were told. The girls from the affluent urban homes were different. They were Europeanised and modern.

When a well-known government minister visited the school for another speech day, he insisted that the musical interludes should be classical European not indigenous tribal music, for which he seemed to have little regard.

A second difference was that the pace and expectations of the school were not so relaxed and timeless. As the country's top girls' school, a great deal was expected of the students, and the teaching staff. They did very well in both O and A level examinations and many went on to university in Kenya, the United Kingdom, the United States and also the Soviet Union. At that time, if not now, the examination results were much better in subjects like English, history, and religious education than in science and mathematics. Too many bright young people then yearned for posts in the civil service when leadership was needed in the real economy.

A third crucial difference was that we had an African head teacher. It was she who rigorously enforced a culture of hard work. Her name was Joan Waithaka. She was the very clever daughter of a Presbyterian minister Musa Gitau and she had attended the Alliance Boys' School between 1944 and 1947 before the girls' school opened.

We were about 6000 feet above sea level and the weather was not tropical throughout the year. There were two rainy seasons and a period of the year known as the grey days. So, when we assembled for school parade on a Monday morning, it was often cold and bleak.

We sang the National anthem.

'O God of all creation

Bless this our land and nation

Justice be our shield and defender

May we dwell in unity

Peace and Liberty

Plenty be found within our borders'

Then Mrs Waithaka would harangue the girls, tell them metaphorically to pull up their socks and work hard. I am sure this was meant to penetrate through to the mostly expatriate teaching staff, who were reminded that they were not in Kenya for a holiday.

I continued to teach African History to the pre-O level students and added to that, nineteenth century British history and World Affairs to A level. To help with the latter, it was helpful to listen to the World Service of the BBC. The girls wondered where I got so much up to date information from.

Indeed, the *Lilly Bolero* signature to the World Service was always a great source of pleasure, keeping us up to date not just with World News but also cultural and sporting events from home.

I did wake up early on June 19 1970 in the belief that they must be profoundly mistaken. We had gone to bed confident that the Labour Government was about to be returned in the general election and here on the radio was some unfortunate aberrant announcing that Mr Heath's Conservatives had been elected.

During 1970 too, we were able to follow the football World Cup in Mexico and a cricket series between England and the Rest of the World, a replacement team for the banned South Africans.

I soon resumed a role that I had had at Kijabe, as organiser and truck driver for the school debating society, visiting schools around the immediate Kiambu District for regular Saturday days out. The students' enthusiasm for debating politics and international affairs far outstripped anything I have ever experienced in this country. They absorbed most of the familiar language and false deference of parliamentary debate and they performed with great verve, humour, and good nature. In the end our best team was invited to do a television programme with the VOK (Voice of Kenya) and I was astonished how easily they adapted to the medium and obviously enjoyed the spotlight.

Kikuyu was not as spectacular a setting as Kijabe but our garden backed on to a series of shamba, small farms growing maize, and we had good friends at both our school and at the Boys' school. From Kikuyu we could drive down to the main Nairobi Road and spent one Saturday afternoon there watching the East African Safari flying past. We went into Nairobi for cricket and to the same club to play bridge at which we made no progress from a very low platform.

People frequently asked us out to dinner in the evening and we liked to take an early breakfast on Sundays with friends at the Norfolk Hotel in Nairobi. Over breakfast we would read the *Observer* paper, flown in very early and then if there was no cricket, we might go off to the horse races. This was something we would not have done at home but there were two courses near Nairobi, both redolent of the recent colonial past. One was in Ngong, near to where Karen Von Blixen, the subject of the *Out of Africa* film, had lived and the other was at Limuru, which was an area that looked like a prosperous suburb in Surrey.

The first time we went to Ngong, Christine put ten Kenya shillings on a horse of little repute and it run home a twenty-to-one winner.

Our contracts with the Kenya Government were officially as Education Officers, so they could call on us to carry out some additional duties. Across the country, in village after village, there was heightened and passionate interest in the public examinations to select the minority who would get the privilege of going to a Secondary school.

I was assigned to run an examination centre close to Kiambu. I knew how anxious the village would be to greet me. I drove to Kiambu to collect the question papers. There were many of us on similar duties, and so it took a little time to find the appropriate parcels for each centre.

I waited until someone came and told me they could not find mine.

'We think you better go and tell them you haven't got them'

'No, I am not going to do that am I? I do not wish to be strung up'

'What shall we do then'?

'You are going back inside and you are going to find them'

And happily, they did!

Christine was expected to give birth towards the end of March. We had arranged for her to go to the Mission Hospital at Kijabe and did not change the arrangement despite the move to Kikuyu. The impending worry however was that the rains were expected in March and I was concerned about the marram road being turned into mud. There were also rumours of a leopard at large near the road. In the event, we did beat the rains by a day or two. Christine went into labour on Sunday 22 March and we got her settled into the hospital by the evening. I stayed with her all that night and was there at the birth of Catherine. By the morning I went round to the McDermott's house to get some sleep. They set off for their day in Nairobi and within about half an hour I was on their bathroom floor, in unbearable pain and vomiting the most wretched green liquid. Suddenly the McDermotts came through the door. They had forgotten something. Mrs McDermott was a GP. She got me into the hospital, I was operated on for acute appendicitis and later on Monday was visited by my wife and our new daughter. The doctors said they thought I would probably have died of peritonitis had my friends not forgotten their shopping list.

By the time Catherine was about a year old, Christine started doing some part time French teaching in Nairobi and so we employed an ayah to do some housework and to look after our daughter. Miriam was a mature lady and brilliant at both the housework and childcare.

We had previously employed a younger woman who came to us with a certificate from a college locally but in time she couldn't really explain to us why she hosed down the ironing board and performed other eccentric domestic duties that were a little superfluous to our needs.

A regular visitor to our home on a Saturday was a student called Nancy Kariuki. One of the difficulties we faced in teaching to the Cambridge Board syllabus on African history is that we had to do a West African paper from about 1000 AD through to 1965. There wasn't a book to cover the breadth of that and so I contracted with a local publisher to write one and that was my project for the second year we were in Kenya.

I planned to write a chapter a week and Nancy came and read it to test its readability for students of her age. I did complete the book; it was sold to schools in Kenya and it is occasionally quoted in higher academic works than O level history.

There was also a small group of girls taking A level French and Christine gave them some help. We both wished them well and were keen to see the papers they actually took.

There was a translation from French into English from some kind of manual for rigging out a sailing boat. This was in an examination set in England for Overseas students, most of whom would never have had any contact with the coast, who, even if they knew of boats, would probably never have come across in English the technical references contained in the passage. How culturally stupid was that? The examination was being taken by intelligent girls from Kisumu, Kakamega and Nyeri not English public-school boys brought up around yacht clubs in Poole Harbour or Weymouth.

My contract ended in December 1971. I cared a great deal about the future prospects of the students I had taught and for their country. We could have tried to stay but there were good reasons why we should now settle in England. There was a general consensus that you either did one tour or you were there until the country finally decided to throw you out. I have followed events in Kenya ever since, sometimes with disappointment but for the most part things appear to have been more stable than they might have been with such a complex ethnic and tribal demographic.

In January 1972 I took up a teaching post in Reading. It was at a bilateral school, called Stoneham in the Tilehurst area of the town. Bilaterals were awful over pragmatic solutions to secondary school organisation, this one having grammar streams and secondary modern streams that separated both pupils and staff. There were some staff with spectacularly conservative opinions. I upset the woodwork teachers by giving an assembly on the civil rights movement in the United States. I listened to a maths teacher who believed the progressive sixties had betrayed those who had died in the second world war. And then there was Norman. Norman used to walk around the staff room at lunchtime intoning an admonitory 'oh yes' which soon exploded into an attack on liberalism and socialism. His favourite prescription was to introduce something similar to the Geddes Axe of the 1920s when Government cuts in expenditure helped to slow down the economy and spread unemployment.

I still thought about Africa whilst we were in Reading. I believed that its successful development, both economically and politically depended on education. I went up to Reading University to talk to its professor of comparative education, Vernon Mallinson, and tried to press on him the importance of Africa. He was totally uninterested and sent me away. Later I did do a Master's Degree in comparative education at London University, via a course at Christ Church College Canterbury. Professor Mallinson attended a seminar on one occasion. His area of study was Belgium and he clearly also saw education in very conservative terms, as a means to re-enforce traditional cultural norms, to emphasize the differences between nations and to solidify institutions and social differentiation. I did not much like him and I exercised my hostility in the master's examination papers with a quite caustic review of his writings.

We left Reading in the summer of 1974.

It was not that we did not enjoy being in Reading. We did and I often have nostalgic feelings about the nearly three years we lived there. We had good friends through the school, especially a very level headed colleague called John Ayre, who was also a good cricketer. We liked the surrounding countryside and after Richard was born in 1972, it was great to go home to the family, after school but sometimes at lunchtime. Occasionally, we would go out for tea at Pangbourne. The girls' school which adjoined Stoneham and with whom we shared a common sixth form timetable, provided some very nice baby sitters and we went out regularly on a Saturday night. I also saw Reading almost upset the then powerful Arsenal side in the FA Cup.

It was good going to football with John Youngman at Chelsea and cricket at Lord's with John Ayre. We had dad down and went to the races at Newbury and we had Chris's family for Christmas. We took dad out to a pub on the way to Wallingford and he asked them if they had 'Bass bitter.' In rural Berkshire that sounded like 'best bitter' and so they said they had. Dad told them in the club that he had had Bass bitter in Reading, though the truth was it was Breakspears' from Henley.

Although I had been appointed as head of history, I really wanted to be in what I might have naively thought to be a more progressive educational environment and after I had read a flattering account of Cyril Poster's community school initiative on the Isle of Sheppey in Kent, we moved there.

I had, and still have, a very profound belief in the importance of education, of policy making and of good school management.

I believe strongly that learning is much more than the acquisition of information, data, and operational skills; it is helping all individuals to think, analyse, be creative and judge maturely what they are being told. It is not just a means of selecting an elite, by putting young people through a series of tests that steadily lead to exclusion. It is not just about achieving qualifications but also developing potential. It gives young people economically transferable skills but it should also open up opportunities for fulfilled lives culturally and recreationally. Schools should be places of moral education, not to impose narrow puritanical personal behaviour but to enhance a sense of social awareness and reflective thought. I find it difficult to believe that if we encourage an educational environment in which school leaders look to their own interest, their own personal reputations and, indeed, their own personal rewards, that schools can then be seen as a good moral guide to their students. Education is a societal process for us all and schools need to be part of their communities, not their own autonomous institutions with their own self interests. My own jaundiced view is that education policy making over recent decades has generally worked against my personal view of how education should be.

PART 2
1974-1997

6

MWALIMU

We moved to the Isle of Sheppey in Kent in 1974.

Christine and I found ourselves a nice newly built house in Wards Hill Road, Minster which needed to be given a name. So, we called it Mwalimu, which is Swahili for Teacher. It is still the official address for that property.

We enjoyed our time in Minster. The beach was only five minutes away. We could walk round to the Glen and we had lots of friends through the school and through my membership of the Gore Court cricket club in Sittingbourne. Christine took the children up the hill to the Methodist Church every Sunday. We had frequent visits from her parents and Owen and Jim also came down with their families. We went out regularly on Saturday nights, thanks to the baby sitters from the school and I could get up to football at Charlton, occasionally Gillingham, and to cricket at Canterbury.

Over the next twenty-one years I taught at Sheppey, then at Penge and finally in Bexley. During that time the profession of teaching and of school management changed fundamentally. In 1974 teachers had considerable control of the curriculum and pastoral care and were strongly influenced by outside administrators in local government and by educational research. This freedom was embodied in the work of the teacher led Schools Council and by teachers' ability to develop their own courses within their schools.

By the end of the 1970s and into the 1980s this teacher autonomy came under strong attack from an approach to public policy based on what protagonists called the provider/consumer split. The theory was that those who provided public services did so in their own interest not in those of the consumer, which in the case of teaching meant the children, parents, and society. In short, we were accused of teaching what we wanted, not what the larger society demanded. We were supposedly experimenting on children to further our own careers and not teaching the 'basics.' Informed educational research was derided as part of the educational establishment. The judges of what was needed were Westminster politicians, goaded on by truculent journalists whose expertise was probably never tested against real experience in schools or with children.

The assault on the 'secret garden' of the education world, of unaccountable teachers and indistinct curriculum was kicked off by the Labour Prime Minister in 1976, Jim Callaghan, in a speech at Ruskin College in Oxford. He raised questions about teaching methods and raised the spectre of a common National Curriculum determined by government.

The political initiative that made education so different by 1995 came however from the right of the political spectrum and was embodied in the Baker Education Act of 1988. This introduced the National Curriculum which not only led to politicians determining the range of subjects taught in schools but also had them trying to influence the precise content. The life cycle of our children was sub divided into key stages and the progress of children would be monitored by testing at these stages. The influence of Local Education Authorities was undermined, something that central government civil servants had always wanted to do, introducing Grant Maintained schools and local management of schools. The role of school governors was greatly enhanced, the schools were expected to be more 'business-like' and an ethos of inter school competition, supported by more parent choice, evolved, as if education was in the market place and not part of a unified national service.

In brief, in 1974 senior school management was focussed principally on the curriculum and individual care for young people. By 1995 it was about budgets, marketing, mission statements and reputation.

The Sheppey Comprehensive School that I worked at from 1974-78 was not like other schools. For a start, the students only joined us at the age of thirteen. The Island had a three- tier system of first schools, middle schools, and the one upper school. It was similar to the then Leicestershire Plan. As the sixth form was relatively small, the vast majority of young people were between the ages of thirteen and sixteen, divided into three age groups with over 500 in each year. This led to a Byzantine system of pastoral care, each year having a year head, four divisional heads and group tutors. On top of these, one of the three-deputy heads had a specific pastoral responsibility. The management of the curriculum was in the hands of heads of departments, with supernumerary heads of faculties and a curriculum deputy head.

There was no school uniform and no school rules.

The school was based on a campus site on slightly raised ground in Minster and it was possible to look out of a teaching window and see the Thames Estuary. This was a pleasant prospect but also a temptation for young people to stroll off campus.

The campus consisted of a series of blocks, four plus the gymnasium and sixth form block. There was one centrally sited with conventional classroom divisions, whilst the other three were pastoral bases for each year group but doubled up as teaching spaces. These were open plan and lent themselves to teaching in abnormally large groups by teams of teachers. For example, we had no specific history or geography classes for year three; instead, they worked through a course of topics that included historical and geographical elements, each of the four divisions at a time with five teachers supervising and monitoring on an individual basis. This was timetabled as humanities. It lent itself to mixed ability teaching, to which many teachers and educationists were committed at the time.

The teaching staff were made up partly of recent recruits who were attracted to the Poster vision for education and local teachers from the previous secondary schools on the Isle of Sheppey, who to a considerable extent, were not attracted to the Poster vision.

Cyril Poster, the headteacher, was an adherent of the community school idea and so wanted us to be a centre of learning for the whole Sheppey community, somewhere to enhance the island identity, to offer cultural opportunities for all age groups and to openly share facilities for the whole population, such as a massive auditorium, a well-stocked library, and a major sports hall.

We had a strong commitment to pastoral care and the need to look at young people as individuals. In so far as we were judged professionally, I suppose our ability to care was equated with our ability to develop learning potential, which was good enough, but a desire to demonstrate caring is not always the same thing as really caring and, in a vast pastoral structure, I sometimes worried that a troubled young person had too many people wanting to be on the case, when individual care is best on a one-to-one basis.

As went with the times, Sheppey School was ready to embrace a myriad of curriculum change and innovation, and I was a great enthusiast for that. We took on much of the work of the Schools Council: the integrated science project (SCISP), Schools Council geography which put social awareness before physical features and Schools Council Social Education. Mathematics was taught through the Kent Maths Project, which was built around individualised learning programmes and was usually taught in the open plan areas.

This was a time when there was still a division between GCE O levels and CSE examinations. The latter allowed teachers to devise their own courses with a considerable amount of teacher assessment but authenticated by the examination boards. These were called Mode 3 s and for about a year teaching staff came to our house in Wards Hill Road and we created a Humanities Mode 3 CSE as an option for students taking courses to 16. At a later school I supported a member of staff who devised a thoughtful course around Angling. It did not just focus on catching fish but also on the social and cultural impact of the pastime and environmental issues.

Unfortunately, the BBC Radio 4 Today programme thought this was a bit risible and their negative coverage also stimulated an Animal Rights march from Crystal Palace to our school gates in Penge.

Finally, Cyril wanted to bring about a different approach to school management, to make it much more consultative and partially democratic.

Early on a Thursday morning, he held open meetings to which any member of staff could go to discuss policy and events. The effect of spreading decision making and influence is that a fluid political environment begins to emerge and, in a school, where so many people held positions of responsibility, power groups competed. The Heads of Faculty were inevitably jealous guardians of their position. This meant the assigned curriculum deputy head was reduced to acting as a technician, doing the timetable but not leading. The pastoral year heads were likewise anxious to assert their position in the school. The difficulty for Poster was that too many of these posts were occupied by teachers inherited from previous Sheppey schools, whilst those more in sympathy with his ambitions were in a more middling tier of management.

In short, there was a great deal of internal politics and it made for stimulating discussion on evenings over a pint in the Ship on Shore, or with wine at dinner parties or at tea in discreet corridors around the campus.

The Sheppey School vision was not helped by the fact that large sections of the community were not sympathetic to its aims. The location of the campus along with the generally poor public transport links did not make it easy to become a centre for community facilities and participation. The caring pastoral ethos along with the lack of uniform and rules, was widely interpreted as too permissive and liberal. The innovative curriculum could be seen as experimenting on our kids, and there was a demand to put a higher priority on achieving better external examination results.

There was, and still is today, a tendency to have lower expectations of the local children than is appropriate for the needs of the youngsters but also the local community and economy.

One helpful initiative for our family was that Poster had set up a nursery in the school that, amongst other positives, would allow some qualified young mothers to return to teaching, at least for some of the time.

So, Christine started to teach French and this had a beneficial impact on our external examination results. Meanwhile, Cath and Rich, who had been born in Reading in 1972, were on the same site with two excellent nursery teachers. Later as they went to a primary school nearby in Halfway, they would come and join us every evening in the staff room and would be generously plied with biscuits by the staff room tea lady.

Whilst Christine was getting students through GCE O level French, I was concentrating on O and A level History. From a very low proportion passing O level history, I was lucky to share classes with a very bright young teacher called Adrian Smith and by 1976 we were getting an over ninety per cent pass rate with a high proportion of grade As. These were specially selected students, the sort who would probably have been selected for Grammar Schools in a different situation, but this was a major step forward and it reflected general progress at that time, with, I remember, comparable striking improvement achieved by other young outsider teachers in English.

I have enjoyed teaching many classes of students in many places, in New Hampshire, Kikuyu, Reading, Bromley, Bexley and Maidstone, but I do not think I have ever found any more enjoyable or rewarding than this successful class on Sheppey in the late 1970s.

I went on courses away from Sheppey, and encountered a patronising even sneering attitude to Sheppey and its comprehensive school. Cynically I sometimes wondered whether in Conservative Kent, which still has an adored selective system, the school at Sheppey was set up to fail. I was always fiercely loyal and did invest a large slice of emotional commitment into the school and the island.

There were manifest shortcomings but things were moving in a positive direction and it could have succeeded. It has not. The social conservatives had their way and appointed a dull replacement when Cyril left to go to Groby in Leicestershire. The uniform came in and talented teachers departed. The brighter students began to take up the option of going to the mainland grammar schools and they in time have been followed by other aspirant families opting for the high schools in Sittingbourne. It is now an Academy but whoever runs it encounters serious problems of teacher recruitment and reputation. I find it very sad. It could have been so much better had the school had more support in the 1970s.

I left Sheppey School in 1978. I was appointed to Kentwood School in Penge and Christine became Head of French at Rowena School in Sittingbourne. We moved to 54 Berkeley Court in Sittingbourne. It has been our home for the last 45 years and where we brought up Cath, Rich and from 1983 John. We have often thought of moving: but we have not done so yet.

In the mid-1960s the Labour Government set out to reform English secondary education into a comprehensive system. In an ideal world that would mean schools serving local communities and recruiting a generally balanced intake of children, in terms of academic ability and potential. In very many cases that did not happen. Some Local Education Authorities delayed long enough to see the return of a Conservative government and kept their overtly selective systems. In places like Bromley, and many others, the intentions behind Labour education policy were undermined by the permissive nature of the 10/65 circular issued by Anthony Crosland. Conscious that there would be strong resistance in local government, he allowed for a myriad of different systems, across the country and within individual authorities.

The principle of parental choice led to schools within an

authority falling into a widely understood pecking order. Parents conscious of which schools had been selective before re-organisation and which had been ill regarded secondary moderns exercised their parental choice as they were expected to do.

The Kentwood School in Penge which I joined in 1978 was not a sought-after school for aspiring parents and had a disproportionate share of less able boys from the Bromley Authority. However, it was housed in the old Beckenham and Penge grammar school building and some parents of higher achieving boys from the then Inner London Education Authority were impressed by this and carrying with them a prejudice against the London Comprehensives brought their sons to Penge.

The bizarre outcome of this jiggery-pokery and some dissembling was a school with the makings of a kind of all ability intake.

The local authority had, it seems, decided to improve this school by adding two senior teachers to the existing senior management of one Head and two Deputies. One was intended to take the curriculum forward, and was flattered with the title of Director of Studies and the other post was to stabilise the pastoral system.

I was appointed Director of Studies.

In a sense, the Head was an important fixture. He had had a good war and was a presence around the place, very often a safety valve for staff struggling with difficult teenager boys. He was a kindly affable man but he was ill qualified to lead a school. He did no teaching and his desk showed no evidence of carrying out any administrative work. It was a very harsh comparison but I thought of him as being a latter-day version of the 1950s Headmaster played by Jimmy Edwards in a Muir and Norden TV comedy called *Whack-O.* Edwards as the Headmaster of Chiselbury had the constant obsequious attention of a deputy called Pettigrew. There was a similar arrangement at Kentwood, whilst the day to day running of the school was administered by a lugubrious but competent second deputy whose response to any idea or innovation was 'the snag is.'

He could see a myriad of snags to my proposal that we could make the sixth form offer better by joining with a nearby girls' school in Anerley, making A levels and vocational courses available through a joint timetable and migrations from school to school. I built up a good working relationship with the head at the girls' school and got the backing of the local Director of Education and Inspectorate and so, despite untold snags, it went ahead.

It was about the only thing I did achieve in my five years there, apart from helping Mr Vickers to establish his controversial Mode 3 CSE course in Angling.

There were a number of very good young teachers at this school and most of them liked cricket. Two especially congenial and intelligent teachers of Geography were Charlie Batteson and Steve Telfer who loved cricket and were very supportive when I tried to promote a more multi ethnic approach to teaching.

One of the most memorable days in Penge occurred in July 1981, when Bob Willis bowled England to victory against Australia at Headingly.

A television was on in the Computer Studies room and all through that memorable spell of bowling boys and teachers from all over the school found a reason to consult the teacher there and to hang around a while out of courtesy. The fall of each wicket was broadcast around the whole school and the celebration at the end of the match was euphoric.

Of course, all this would not get a commendation from Ofsted but it created a bond around a tough school, bringing together teachers and boys in a moment of celebration. And that was a good thing.

Whilst I was at Penge, I used to travel up to the London University Institute of Education every Monday for a couple of years. I was awarded an MA in Comparative Education, writing a dissertation on Secondary School organisation, using examples of structures from a wide range of countries, including the USA, Russia, Germany, and Sweden.

Whilst Christine and I were teaching, Cath and Rich were attending Minterne primary school, which is only a five-minute walk from our home. Rich liked playing football and Cath was good at gymnastics. In the evenings, I liked to read them extracts from the ludicrous *Jennings at School* novels by Anthony Buckeridge, stories that had been popular radio programmes in my childhood. Jennings and his mate Darbyshire had two contrasting teachers, a calm Mr Carter, and an irascible and impatient Mr Wilkins, played by Wilfred Babbage. Mr Babbage was the uncle of the girl who had taken me to Woolwich Town Hall to support her mum in a local election.

I moved on from Kentwood in 1983. By that time my dad had died, from old age. His later years had been good for him, being in regular contact with all our families. My brothers' wives and Christine were very kind and he saw a lot of his grandchildren, something sadly my mum never got to do. The last time I saw him alive I wanted to give him a hug but we did not do that sort of thing. I wish I had.

In May 1983, I was interviewed for the post of Deputy Head at Bexley Erith Technical High School. It was the most professional and thorough selection process I had so far experienced. It took two days and it involved a variety of challenges. I thought it was rather good and was very pleased to be appointed. It could not have been a bad move because I stayed there for twelve years.

I started at BETHS in September 1983 and in November Christine gave birth to John. By this time Cath was thirteen and Rich eleven, and so John was to have quite a lot of parental and quasi parental support in his early years. The secondary school system in Sittingbourne at that time was called the Thameside Scheme, another elegant detour around circular 10/65. It involved all students joining High Schools at eleven but with a selected minority transferring to the two single sex grammar schools at thirteen. Cath was already at Highsted Girls school and Rich was to join Borden Boys grammar school in due course. They both achieved good academic results at these schools but we had doubts about the breadth of education provided and the quality of individual pastoral care. John also went to Borden later on. My impression from attending parent evenings for both the boys was of some unacceptably poor teaching especially in history, with dictated notes, poor feedback, and a lack of understanding of new assessment techniques, around the use of documents and the skills of understanding and interpretation.

Cath and Rich both belonged to a local athletics club that made them feel at home. In their teens they got a lot of support and friendship from the Methodist Church youth club and the thoughtful Sunday night Chat Clubs run by our good friend the Minister Bill Prince and by Pat and Derek Goodger.

Rich had also shown signs from an early age of being good at football. We had seen him running rings round other cub scouts and so he joined a local colt's side. He was a year younger than most of the side and so we accepted that he might not get a regular place. Sadly, he turned up every Sunday throughout the winter, all changed and ready but hardly got a chance to play. One week he did come on as a substitute, scored a spectacular goal and was left on the sideline the following week. The problem? He was small for his age at that time and the guy running the team obviously believed the bigger boys would be more likely to win the games and the plastic trophies at the end of the season. For me, paternal disappointment was mixed with an irritable conviction that English football has always been held back by an obsession with physical strength and endeavour, when, in the end, it is skill and imagination that really matters. I like to think that attitude has changed in this country, with people like Trevor Brooking and Gareth Southgate, as it were, moving the goalposts. As an adult, Rich had a lot of success on the football field.

The Headmaster at BETHS was John Tobin and the other deputy was Jim Sheath. John Tobin was energetic and dedicated to the school. He was a very good physics teacher and did more teaching than was the norm for a secondary school leader. Jim and I also had fairly full timetables. Jim taught engineering drawing.

He had been on bombing missions over Germany in the Second World War, had a deep knowledge of art and architecture and had a conservative scepticism directed particularly at the Guardian newspaper. He took a fairly libertarian view that too much care and protection of the individual only led to impoverishment of the soul. Humans living a real life have to suffer the consequences of their free will, as well as experiencing joy. We were not quite on the same page but his sense of humour and tolerance made him good company.

Change did come about in the 1980s and we often shared doubts about that change, though from differing perspectives. It was argued quite rightly that we should value young people for more than just examination results. However, unable to get out of the mindset that value had to be demonstrated by some form of official record, the powers that be, promoted the idea of young people keeping records of achievement, wrapped up in an ostentatious cover. I rather felt that respect and empathy needed to be built in more inter-personal ways.

Our staff, and the staff of other local schools, were gathered into our hall and one of our Bexley Inspectors, a good man, was charged with persuading us of the virtues of records of achievement. After about an hour and half of unctuous platitudes, the rest of the teaching staff broke into inevitable discussion groups and the three of us adjourned to the Head's office. John Tobin asked us what we thought. I launched into a bit of a diatribe.

Jim was asked for his reaction. His laconic reply indicated his level of interest in the topic.

'Aren't our Inspectors paid enough to turn up in a decent pair of trousers?'

The boys did not want to be bothered completing these worthless things and too much time and resource was wasted on them.

I did have a look at one completed by a fifth year boy. There was a section on problem solving, which he had dutifully, and I think seriously, completed.

The problem it transpired was that he had a tendency to arrive late for school. He had however solved this problem by catching an earlier bus.

My initial responsibility was to lead on pastoral care. In reality, there were some good year heads in place and it was not an onerous task. However, in the first few weeks I did take charge of a number of twelve-year-old boys who were finding it difficult to leave their mums at the school gate and whose mums were asking us to 'give him time to get used to it'. That meant taking the boys back home, which was really not a good idea.

On one occasion, I did persuade one tearful refuser that he should stay, go to the PE lesson, and then meet me afterwards to see how he felt.

The lesson was a cross country run. I met him as planned

though he was still tearful.

'Did you manage to do the run?'

'Yes'

'Oh well done, I am very pleased with you. Do you know what position you came'?

'Yes'

'And what was it '?

'First'

He stayed for seven years and was one of the school's best sportsmen.

The school was popular with parents, especially it seemed with policemen. I had several visits from one particular constable complaining about the bullying of his son by a group of boys. It was not easy to tell him that it was his son who was the bully, that the group of boys were of a very passive nature and that they were the ones being terrorised.

The school was calm, almost serene. The behaviour of boys around the school was good, though their language in the playground was a bit robust.

Then a few weeks into my first term there, tragedy struck. A third-year boy, with a reputation for recklessness, accidentally hung himself whilst experimenting with a noose he had seen on a TV programme. John Tobin, who had a well disguised but profound emotional side, was utterly devastated and we naturally experienced pressure from parents and press.

Then, by the beginning of the following week, the Head

had to travel to Bristol to see his ailing father. During the Wednesday lunch hour, I had to go down to the front office to see a distraught sixth form student. He said he thought his friend, another sixth former, was dead. We went down to the side of the small local river and his fears were realised. I sent a message back to Jim Sheath to alert the police and the local authority, whilst I sat with the poor boy who had died and the other poor boy who had persuaded his friend to sniff glue for the first time.

By the time I got back to the school and had spoken to the Chief Education officer and responded to phone calls, John Tobin had returned.

It was an awful time for him and the whole school. He said later that he had not been totally sure about my appointment but that I had earned his regard through these difficult times.

These were not the only times we had to work our way through difficult situations. We became aware of accusations of criminally inappropriate sexual activity by a member of staff with boys in the school. I was sent to collect the teacher in question, who was shaking as I accompanied him to the office. He was subsequently committed to prison.

Later on, we were concerned that a generally conscientious teacher had absented himself for a long period of time, saying he was ill but offering no evidence of that illness. I went to his home in Dartford and he confessed that he did not want to come to school because he was under investigation for importing child pornography from Europe.

These incidents do not give a fair picture of a tranquil and generally happy school but they happened.

I enjoyed my teaching there. If you teach a fairly full timetable as a Deputy Head, you can tend to pick up the loose threads, so in addition to my usual subject history, I taught English, economics, politics, general studies, and study skills. I also took groups of sixth formers on a residential course to inner London, to see a different side of life to that of suburban Bexley. We stayed in a Church of England hostel across the river from the Houses of Parliament and over three days visited a multi ethnic primary school in the Old Kent Road, the Brixton Leisure Centre, the Brixton Police station, with a gruesome array of vicious weapons and a building site across the river. In the evening we went to see the musical *Blood Brothers*. We did this on a few occasions and the boys appreciated it and performed enlightening presentations back in Bexley, but it was only the boys who were pre-disposed to examining social differences who opted to go. The expeditions were therefore not transformative.

They were old enough to look after themselves and one evening I told them I was off over to the House for a meeting with Paddy Ashdown. This was in the early 1990s. I was a Parliamentary candidate for the Liberal Democrats and served on two policy making working parties, one on sports policy, the other, more seriously on the economy. I went over to Westminster to present the first to the party's Federal Policy Committee. It was chaired by Paddy Ashdown. At seven pm he said most authoritatively that all the business, it was not just sport, would be concluded by nine pm, that he would allow no digressions or special pleading. We finally got on to my policy at a quarter to ten and finished about a quarter past.

On the subject of Paddy Ashdown, we had a visit at BETHS one afternoon from the local MP and former Prime Minister, Ted Heath. He talked to the sixth form boys about the importance of Europe to their futures. He claimed that but for the oil crisis of 1973, he, 'Georges' (Pompidou) and 'Helmut' (Schmidt) would have created a new prosperous, secure, and democratic Europe,

The boys were not very interested.

When we retired for tea, I asked Heath for his opinion on Paddy Ashdown,

'Very nice chap but no politician. Too nice to his opponents.'

He also talked most affectionately about Harold Wilson.

As I indicated before, whilst I was happy enough teaching in the classroom, I was part of a senior management team and we were subject to the educational zeitgeist that reached its peak in the 1988 Baker Education Act, with its National Curriculum, its Key Stage testing, and its drive towards Grant Maintained school status.

I cannot say that there had not been problems that needed to be solved in education. I would not deny that the emphasis on testing and results has helped children of average ability. I suspect too that the teaching profession is now more professional than it was in the 1970s when there were a few lead swingers about. However, I was uncomfortable with the whole drift towards centralised and political control, to a narrowing of educational objectives and to an environment, that seemed to me to encourage a spirit of self- centred competition between schools within the system. My reaction may have been extreme but that is how I felt.

I did go on a couple of interviews to be a headmaster myself. Apart from my own shortcomings, I was not going to get anywhere because I could not enthuse around the questions being asked, which were all part of the conservative zeitgeist.

As deputy head with a responsibility around the school finances, I had to attend dreary governors' meetings, with people who believed, because of their own career backgrounds, they had something special to offer. For the most part, they had not. I remember one long and tedious evening in 1994, when I could only sustain myself by wondering how Charlton had done in an FA Cup away match at Blackburn, at that time one of the strongest sides in the country. I got in the car to great relief at about ten o'clock. Cup shock! One-nil to Charlton, Pitcher the scorer.

Then by the mid-1990s, the governors decided that it would be in the interests of the school to apply for Grant Maintained status. The Government were offering financial incentives for schools to transfer from local authorities to central government control and to be able to exercise a greater degree of semi-autonomy. I did not like this. I took a very hostile line, telling the very likeable chair of governors that the school was not his to cast away in such a fashion, that it was part of the local community and should recognise its responsibilities to other schools in the area. Of course, I was not going to win.

I do make very abrupt decisions. One weekend in 1995, I rang John Tobin and said I wanted to resign. I taught later in adult education and at the Maidstone Girls Grammar School but my career was at a finish.

I did return to BETHS to present the prizes at their annual speech day and made the keynote speech, so there were no hard feelings. Over the twelve years I had been at the school I had delivered many assembly sermons, often of an unconventional kind. They were happy for me to do so, one more time.

I had often drafted these assemblies in my head whilst making the journey to Bexley from Sittingbourne on the wretchedly congested A2. They may have come across as spontaneous because that is what they were.

If I had no assembly to think about, I regularly listened to the *BBC Radio 4 Today* programme. There were three politicians who forced me to switch off, not through constructive censorship but just instinctively. One was the British Prime Minister Margaret Thatcher. Another was the mendacious Serb Leader Radovan Karadzic, and the third was the slightly obsequious Shadow Home Secretary Tony Blair. Just as we remember the moment we heard of Kennedy's death in Dallas, so I can remember exactly the time and place when I heard that Mrs Thatcher had resigned. As to Tony Blair, my opinion nuanced over time.

The decision to end my teaching career so precipitously on policy grounds reflects the fact that I was too much into politics by the mid-1990s. I made many political speeches on education. I was nominally the Lib Dems spoken on education for the south east. I had publicly opposed Grant Maintained schools and the rest of the ideological stuff. I had done so in a speech at a Liberal Democrat Conference. Nobody probably cared at all but to me it did not feel right to be part of this kind of school takeover. It was a political decision to resign and there was no advantage in it, either for myself or my family.

By 1995 Cath and Rich were both university graduates: Cath in French from Sheffield and Rich in Politics and International Affairs from Southampton. John was still in Secondary School but eventually took a degree in Sports Science from Durham and an MSc and PhD from Exeter. For my part I was not at all sure what I was going to do henceforth but I found a path and it involved politics, which had started back in 1980.

7

THE MOULD SURVIVES

As I move into the latter parts of this memoir, my politics takes a more central role than before.

During my Liberal Democrat days, I was still teaching and roaming around watching youthful cricket.

After 1997, my teaching was confined to a short spell of part-time A level politics with the talented and exceptionally untidy girls at Maidstone Grammar. I did have a new go at managing a Kent youth side but that finished by 2004, the last year too that I played cricket.

Family was central to our lives but for outside interests over the last twenty years, politics assumed a prominence I had not anticipated.

Of course, we have a considerable literature from the memories of prominent Westminster politicians and from lauded journalists, but rarely, if ever, does anyone pay attention to the observations and experience of someone active at the grassroots of politics and from life in local government

I had always been interested in politics, at least from the age of about ten and always supported the Labour Party. However, for some time I had thought there was common ground and a potentially a large constituency of support between the mainstream centre of the Labour Party and the more socially progressive wing of the Liberal Party. By the 1970s, like many others, I was prepared to vote tactically. So, in 1974, I voted Liberal in Reading and in 1979 voted Labour in the Faversham constituency, which then covered Sittingbourne and Sheppey.

I was disappointed by the election result in 1979 and felt the path taken by Labour over the years that immediately followed was not going to end in electoral success. It is still the case that in my lifetime only three Labour leaders have won General Elections and they all did so by augmenting the core Labour vote with a message to floating voters; Attlee with an appeal to a unifying patriotism, Wilson with a desire for modernisation in both the economy and society and Blair by appealing to elements of social conservatism. Blairism involved a sophisticated combination of communitarianism and policy triangulation. It also apparently required writing for the Daily Mail and travelling miles to talk to Murdoch.

For most of the post war period, the Conservative Party had gone along with the consensus to limit unemployment, to support a mixed economy and to accept the need for tax funded public services including a comprehensive welfare state. Those parts of their party that disagreed with this were largely treated as an eccentric minority. This consensus was labelled Butskellism, a combination of instincts represented by Butler from the left of the Conservative Party and Gaitskell from the right of the Labour Party.

1979 saw the end of this consensus. Reducing taxes,

cutting public services, privatising core sections of the economy, disregarding the impact of policy on employment, emasculating trade unions, making the state smaller and weakening local government prevailed over traditional Conservatism and as the new Prime Minister was seen as an embodiment of that change, the prevailing right-wing consensus was called Thatcherism. It remains a strong influence in British politics. Some people seem to get promoted to senior positions in government, for no other reason than their loyalty to this ideology.

The Labour Party response to this in 1980 was to try to tack smartly to the left and to experience a first wave of entryism from Trotskyite activists.

I felt I ought to do something. Early in 1980 I was preparing our Sunday lunch when a sudden impulse struck me. Around the corner from me was a man called Tony Aldous and I walked round and knocked on his door. He had stood for the Liberal Party in the 1979 election and I asked him if he would like to recruit me. Interestingly, it was not long before he joined the Labour Party. It can be very fluid on the left of British politics.

Why? I had always been Labour. My views have never really changed. I believe that well -funded public services paid for by progressive taxation act benignly to redistribute life chances for people and where they do not, we should intervene to tackle inequalities, especially in health and education. However, apart from having doubts about the electability of the Labour Party, there were three broader issues that made me prepared to give the Liberal Party a go. They had a much clearer commitment to working with the European Community than Labour; a strong belief in elections by proportional representation; and a seemingly greater awareness of the need to protect the environment from excessive industrial production of carbon dioxide and chlorofluorocarbons. In 2023 it is quite possible to subscribe to all three and be at home in the Labour Party, or nearly so.

I was invited to my first local Liberal meeting. I thought I ought to prepare myself so I was not found wanting. I read up quite a bit about Liberal approaches to the economy and especially their support for mutualism, with greater worker interest in the companies they work for.

In the event, the meeting had a somewhat narrower focus. In brief, two people, one of them Tony Aldous, debated for over an hour or so, the principles behind a proposed leaflet advising people how they might contact a well-known company in the event of their sewer being blocked. The Aldous view, remembering he was about to join the Labour Party, was that the Liberal Party should not be seen to be promoting a private sector interest. The contrary view came from Peter Morgan, a previous Parliamentary candidate, whose whole soul was dedicated to providing local community support. Over the years, I learned a lot about winning local backing from Peter who, for the most part, scrupulously avoided offending anyone by sublimating his opinions on national political matters.

The local party was pedestrian and parochial. Election campaigning was dire and built exclusively on Peter's well-earned reputation, which was not much use for other candidates.

Without much optimism I agreed to become the Constituency Chairman. Then in 1981 the Social Democrat Party (SDP) emerged from divisions in the Labour Party. For a short while this raised hopes that there might be a 'breaking of the mould' of British politics. The first wave of hope was largely extinguished by the general election of 1983.

The mould to be broken was the parliamentary dominance by two parties and the election of majoritarian governments based on the support from a minority of voters. Mould breaking required the introduction of a genuine multiparty democracy on a European model with voting through a more democratic system of proportional representation. To get to that point, a third force needed to make significant gains in Westminster in the existing structure. In the early 1980s this seemed plausible, after a decade of semi dysfunctional government and a tendency of both the Labour Party and the Conservatives to move towards their extremes. The emergence of the SDP owed much to a disruptive and divisive Labour Conference at Wembley in 1981 whilst the Conservatives were increasingly in thrall to a neo liberal ideology that was at odds with many of their one nation instincts. A third party could attract support from both main parties.

The SDP impetus, as I recall, started with a television lecture in memory of Richard Dimbleby, given by the President of the European Commission and former Deputy Leader of the Labour Party, Roy Jenkins. His strong European credentials had much to do with the split from the then Labour Party.

He said,

'As a forum of national debate, the House of Commons has declined. The great clashes of party principle and the conflicting convictions of major personalities have mostly given way to a sterile exchange of unconvincing slogans and recrimination, to a background of unedifying noise.'

This rung many bells and was taken up by the media, including both broadsheet and tabloid newspapers.

The SDP was formally launched in March 1981, when Jenkins, joined other grand former Labour MPs, Shirley Williams, William Rogers, and David Owen, at the latter's house to agree the Limehouse Declaration with an outline programme of electoral reform, support for a mixed economy, and backing for European integration. Moderate and centrist was how it was described by the media.

A launch meeting was organised in Sittingbourne for those wanting to join the new party and members of the Liberal Party were invited along. The meeting was addressed by Dick Taverne, who on his own had won a by election in Lincoln in 1973, calling himself a Social Democrat. He was joined on the front table by various potential local leaders, one of whom was a farmer called Tom Ledger, who I knew from cricket. He was to play a major part in local government, leading Swale Borough Council with great good sense in the 1990s.

Roy Jenkins for the SDP and David Steel for the Liberal

Party soon determined to work together in an Alliance of two parties. Opinion polls soon indicated very strong support for this Alliance and for the virtue of working together. At the Liberal Conference in 1981 at Llandudno, Steel was even emboldened enough to tell his delegates to go back to their constituencies and prepare for government. Famous by-elections were won in Crosby by Shirley Williams and in Glasgow Hillhead by Jenkins, whilst the less celebrated Bill Pitt had already won for the Liberals in Croydon North West, supported, though not necessarily decisively, by campaigners from Sittingbourne.

Breaking the Mould either had to be done swiftly or it was going to be a long frustrating journey possibly with no end. The SDP/Liberal Alliance needed a significant breakthrough in the 1983 General Election. In the event only twenty three seats were won despite a strong popular vote, which naturally led to a call for electoral reform and a fairer system. The seats won lent on areas of traditional Liberal support and the SDP garnered only six seats. After so much euphoria, this was a profound setback for those who wanted to see change.

The Falklands War of 1982 had changed the political climate and had benefited the Tory Prime Minister Margaret Thatcher in particular. However, with the benefit of hindsight, I do not think that was the only reason for the demise of SDP and Liberal ambitions in 1983.

At the time, as a Liberal member, I fully supported the idea of an alliance, in which, two parties shared out seats in order of supposed winnability. In Kent, a priority list was drawn up, and like school children picking their sides for a playground game of football, the Liberals had first choice and selected Maidstone and then the two parties took the lead in alternating constituencies. Ours was then Faversham, and being number four in the pecking order it fell to the SDP to select the parliamentary candidate. Both parties then campaigned for the candidate that one party selected. We backed Mark Goyder the erudite SDP candidate in both 1983 and 1987.

He worked exceptionally hard and came second on both occasions, but through no fault of his own, got nowhere near beating the Conservatives.

My retrospective view now is that when it came to a real general election, rather than by- elections, the voters returned to the simplicity of trying to vote for a single party government, that they found the notion of a two-party alliance unviable and that they wanted to know if they voted for the Alliance who might be Leader or in extremis the Prime Minister. Calling Roy Jenkins 'Prime Minister Designate' was not going to work and this rather haughty description spoke of a disconnect between the parties and many voters.

It was not going to happen like that.

To maintain the momentum that the SDP had in 1981, which was partly based on passing fashion, they might have been better advised not to go into such a complete arrangement with the Liberal Party, to have recognised areas of Liberal strength but to have offered themselves as the only alternative opposition in many constituencies. I would not have said that at the time.

There is no guarantee that that would have made a difference. As we found when campaigning, and not for the first or last time, the Conservatives were very good at frightening people into the belief that voting 'Alliance' might 'let in' Labour with its odd 1983 Manifesto.

After all the bidding and negotiation, neither SDP or Liberals got anywhere near winning a seat in Kent, nor since have the Liberal Democrats.

After the 1983 election, I believed the project had one more chance, that the two parties now had to unite and a clear leader identified in the public mind. It did not happen. There were policy issues between the two parties, over nuclear disarmament for example. David Owen became the Leader of the SDP and his working relationship with David Steel was presumed to be uneasy. This was painfully enhanced by a cruel but brilliant *Spitting Image* sketch in which a domineering David Owen tells a wimpish David Steel that the two parties should be combined with the name of the new party being a combination of the two, with Social Democrat being taken from the SDP and Party from the Liberals, and the Leadership being taken from the name Owen in the SDP and David from the Liberals.

We all worked very hard again for our Alliance candidates in the 1987 general election. This time we lost votes and one seat. The Labour Party was in the process of restoration from its 1983 mire. The chance to break the mould had been lost and possibly squandered by tribal considerations in two parties that advertised themselves as being above such things.

It was now going to be the long haul. The following year

the merger of the two parties belatedly took place but not with David Owen and a few others who tried to continue with a separate SDP until they were beaten by the Raving Loony Party in a by-election. The new party was from the start more Liberal than SDP. Many Social Democrats returned to the Labour Party, especially once Blair and Brown took over the leadership, and after being called the Social and Liberal Democrats, ridiculed as the Salads, it became the Liberal Democrats.

I had attended the Blackpool Conference in January when the Liberal Party agreed to seek merger with the SDP. There were some standard speeches from people like David Steel and Paddy Ashdown but the most memorable line came from Ludovic Kennedy.

'Of course, we are going to merge. Why else would we come to this bleak watering hole in the middle of winter if we are not going to do so?'

The new party's early days were abysmal and polling support very low, but there were sound foundations at local levels and Paddy Ashdown was an effective Leader.

These were the days when I was still driving to school in Bexley, listening to the BBC Today programme, censoring Mrs Thatcher. I was amazed and encouraged by the number of times Ashdown got slotted into the programme and I understand that was because he regularly got up very early in the morning and offered to be interviewed.

He did very well too, in the early difficult days, raising party morale at Annual Conferences and getting round to members at Regional Conferences too. It was a pity that he and his advisers just got the 1997 election wrong.

Ashdown privately understood that breaking the mould meant electoral reform; electoral reform required agreement with one of the major parties and some form of coalition; and to Ashdown the only option was the Labour Party. In Tony Blair he found a courteous listener and contingent arrangements were put in place, subject to the 1997 election creating the right circumstances for working together.

It did not. The Liberal Democrats won forty six seats, a leap forward by most standards but too small a number to press Labour, with a landslide majority, to do more than offer token efforts to change the system.

Understandably, but fatally, the Liberal Democrats, had underestimated the swing against the Conservatives, targeted too few seats and allowed many that could have had party support to fall nicely into the laps of the Labour Party.

After 1997, they continued to play a serious part in Westminster politics, even if not in mould breaking fashion. They found distinctive ground in 2005 through their opposition to the Iraq War. Kennedy was a popular leader but by the 2010 election, the leadership had moved to the right, re-asserting traditional liberal economic thinking, and becoming less of a social democratic party. It was not surprising that Clegg chose the Conservatives as coalition partners, the results largely prescribed it, but it did not lead to a genuine drive for electoral reform and since 2015 the Liberal Democrats have been fighting the negative impact of supporting a Tory government, which amongst other things introduced a destructive approach to the NHS, plus general austerity in public services.

However, recent by election results suggest that the stigma of 2010-2015 has abated and the Liberal Democrats may have a significant role to play after the next general election.

Or, it could be 1997 over again.

Throughout the years up to 1997, I had supported the party by contesting both local and parliamentary elections.

I was elected as a Liberal/SDP councillor on the Swale Borough Council in 1987, winning in the Borden village ward, generally assumed to be safe Conservative. I won again in 1991, largely campaigning alone with Christine's help. I did however, recruit one useful supporter, a grammar school boy who lived in the ward with a strong interest in politics. He was called Mike Baldock.

From 2019-2022 I led the Swale Council and Mike Baldock was our deputy leader. He then led the Council for a year and successfully maintained the ruling coalition. He is well qualified in the sense that he has from time to time been a member of all the factions in the Swale Coalition.

The results were in 1987

Truelove	Lib/SDP Alliance	610
Fuller	Conservative	413
Donnellan	Labour	74

And 1991

Truelove	Liberal Democrat	747
Fuller	Conservative	224
Eagle	Labour	49

Both these results illustrate the ease with which a third party can squeeze one of the main major parties out of contention in a local government election. A significant number of Labour supporters would have voted for me to keep out the Tories.

By the early 1990s, the Council was finely divided between three groups, the Tories, Labour, and the Liberal Democrats. The positions of responsibility were roughly split three ways and for a time I was Chair of the Health and Environment committee. So, with a good leader in Tom Ledger, we were exercising some real political authority and it is not surprising that here, and in many parts of the country, Liberal Democrats put local government and local elections above Westminster politics, unless members lived in the minority of genuine target parliamentary seats.

The Chair of Health and Environment soon offered me the dubious opportunity of fronting up a public meeting, followed by TV cameras, called because Swale Council had allowed the building of part of an estate on contaminated land. I also appeared in a TV programme about air pollution from our steelworks in Sheerness. There was also a high-profile campaign to try to save Acute Medical Services at the small Sheppey General Hospital in Minster.

By 1992, I was the parliamentary candidate for the Liberal Democrats in our local constituency of Faversham. I knew there was little chance of winning but I had really joined a political party to campaign on national matters. I had found the fact that we were compelled to accept an SDP only shortlist in 1983 and 1987 frustrating and I was bursting with things to say publicly on a wide range of topics, especially the economy, environment, health, and education.

I got accustomed to having, at least locally, a high media profile, which could be fun. The local papers were generous. In October 1990 I took a group of local activists down to Eastbourne for a by-election. During the week of the election, I rang BBC Radio Kent and told them to expect a major upset. They scoffed. So, I said if I am right, you will interview me on Friday morning, is that agreed? It was. The Liberal Democrat candidate David Bellotti won with fifty-one per cent of the vote. From that time onward, BBC Radio Kent continually used me as the go to Liberal Democrat in Kent. I appeared on a number of Budget specials, on one of which Anne Widdicombe remarked that I did not know what I was talking about.

During the election campaign of 1992, they organised a discussion between all the candidates standing in Faversham. I quite liked both the Tory Roger Moate and the Labour candidate, Helen Brinton and we also had a candidate from the Natural Law party standing in the cause of peaceful meditation. Helen was sometimes a little agitated and thought she might benefit from a verbal assault on both Mr Moate and myself and when I was asked to respond I suggested she went into alliance with

Natural Law and calmed down.

The Eastbourne by- election was not the only one we supported for the wider party. We set out very early one morning in 1993 and drove to Newbury in West Berkshire. Our agent, Bob Dolan, came with us. He expected a lot from canvassers and it was not until about eight in the evening that we gave up trying to win the support of the stable lads at Lambourn. Midway through the afternoon in a very prosperous village somewhere west of Newbury, he directed me up a very steep hill towards a well-appointed property.

'Surely, they are Tory Bob, I pleaded'

To no avail.

When I reached the summit of this considerable hill, the elderly owner with a rather posh voice told me there was no chance of his voting Liberal Democrat.

'I am Labour. I voted for you last time for tactical reasons and it didn't work. I am not going to do that again.'

We also went to Winchester, Christchurch and Eastleigh, all striking by-election successes. In Christchurch I was sent out in the middle of the afternoon on election day and met an irate lady who said she had voted Liberal Democrat but would not in future if we insisted on delivering polling day reminders at four o'clock in the morning.

~

I especially enjoyed being invited by Radio Kent on to an Election Special programme for the Kent County Council elections in 1994. Before we went on air at ten o'clock, they gave us a generous glass of wine. This was topped up regularly over the next few hours, balanced by occasional cups of coffee. I had played a key part in organising the three campaigns in the Sittingbourne divisions and we won all three. There was a Labour lady on the panel who was especially generous in acknowledging the Liberal Democrat gains. For the first and only time, the Conservatives lost control in Kent and the Liberal Democrat and Labour County Councillors formed an effective administration. I came home from the Chatham studios at three in the morning in a contented state.

~

The anchor for all these programmes and interviews was a very professional journalist who lived on Sheppey, called Colin Johnson. He changed career paths in time and has been Chaplain to a Mayor on our Council.

In the 1992 general election, we came third just a few votes behind Labour. I might have been wise to bank that and do something else but I stood again in 1997 in what was now the Sittingbourne and Sheppey constituency, with Labour's Derek Wyatt taking the seat from Tory MP Roger Moate, who had been there for twenty-seven years.

The Labour Party had done well to select Wyatt for this constituency. He had an easy-going approachability that over three general elections not only secured the Labour vote, but also sustained support from floating, independent, and locally focussed voters. Roger Moate, the departing Conservative MP had privately confided to me during the election campaign that I seemed to be well to the left of Derek Wyatt. I did not respond.

The results were

1992

Moate	Conservative	32,755
Brinton	Labour	16,404
Truelove	Liberal Democrat	15,896

1997

Wyatt	Labour	18,723
Moate	Conservative	16,794
Truelove	Liberal Democrat	8,447

These results again indicate how easily a third-party candidate gets squeezed, unless the party both nationally and locally has tried seriously to convince voters that there is a viable chance of winning.

Notwithstanding, the 1992 campaign had been fun, by and large. Tom Ledger provided a battle bus, decorated in party colours, logo, and my name which we drove around to our canvass venues. John was not too pleased when we turned up at his school gates to collect him one afternoon in the battle bus.

I campaigned at least six hours every day and then worked for a couple more on press releases and briefings to activists. Most days there was a good team out and we frequently had a lunch party at home of fish and chips. Of the 1997 campaign, I can recall little with fondness. Local campaigners came out but that was in large part because there were also county council elections taking place. I can remember one good night canvassing in the Roman ward where George Colvin was Councillor, only for him to reveal that he had deliberately chosen to send me only to gilt edged certainties, just to keep my morale up. At the count, the only interest was in whether Derek Wyatt had won. Christine and I walked around rather aimlessly. We started to move towards one set of counting tables with boxes from somewhere on Sheppey. Richard and John stopped us.

'Don't go there dad,' said Rich.

'Why, have I not got many votes?'

'No dad, you haven't got any votes'

After 1992, I had thought of not standing a second time. However, I went off to Oxford for a two-day assessment of candidates for the fast stream, what another party calls the A list. I was told by an assessor that I scored above all the other candidates and should look for a winnable seat. Living where I was, I had no idea where that would be and I really could not envisage disrupting the family. So, I agreed to stand again locally, in what was a slightly smaller Sittingbourne and Sheppey constituency. It was not a sound decision.

I campaigned a lot in my constituency. I am always a little amused by politicians of all parties who claim support for their policies on the doorstep. I have always found it desperately difficult to get people to actually discuss policy on their doorsteps.

I got instead,

'I will vote for you because I don't like party politics'

'But we are a political party'

'But not a proper one'

Or,

'I'm voting Liberal Democrat to get out of Europe' a somewhat misconceived position but one that was adamantly maintained

Or, when trying to draw attention to my position on health, and my distrust of NHS Trusts, I got this response from a lady in Sittingbourne

'I need the NHS because of problems with my back passage'

'Isn't that a housing matter'?

'No, you know'

'Oh, I see'

During the period between these two elections, I played a more active role in the party outside my home area.

Immediately after the 1992 election we had a debrief at Westminster with Paddy Ashdown and others and I began the evening by saying elections depend on having a viable economic policy message and that we did not have one. Paddy Ashdown handed over to Alan Beith who talked about the success of promising to 'put a penny on income tax to pay for education' which did not really qualify as an adequate answer.

On another occasion I made a speech in the same mode, about us having no clearly defined education policy. Paddy Ashdown said it was a good speech but flawed in one respect,

'We do have an education policy and I wrote it'

I worked on two Policy working groups. The first was on Sports Policy which, after taking it to the Federal Policy meeting at Westminster, I proposed its adoption to the party Conference at Nottingham. It was at the Spring Conference and I was down to speak at a quarter to five on a Saturday afternoon. It seemed that the party was viscerally divided between those who thought sport mattered and those who, perhaps because of unhappy schooldays, hated it.

At this time on a Saturday afternoon the sports fans went off to hear the football results and the haters remained in the Conference. I referred to John Major's love of cricket and his ability to foster balls up here and balls up there. We got the policy through but only after a few vitriolic speeches in opposition.

Apart from speaking about education at the Scarborough Conference, I had also made a speech at Glasgow on the economy and got on to the Federal Policy Working Party to devise a more coherent approach.

Being on the Economic Policy working party was much more fulfilling than sport. There were many distinguished members in the group. It was expertly chaired by Margaret Sharp, now Baroness Sharp of Guildford; expert in the sense that she was professionally a successful economist and also expert as a chair, harnessing a diversity of views and placating some fairly arrogant individuals. Part of the group, including the chair, were essentially social democrats in favour of greater government intervention in the free market. Others were more economically liberal and some wanted to devote a lot more time to discussing corporate law than I welcomed.

Agreed policies emerged, mostly with Margaret's signature on them. First was the introduction of a central bank with the power to set interest rates independently of the Treasury. Second was a fiscal strategy that involved balancing the revenue budget but borrowing for investment. Third was a drive to tackle productivity through investment, innovation, and education, with government taking the lead.

The policies were a decisive advance on where the party had been in 1992 but there was one emerging difficulty. As the 1997 election approached, it was obvious that Labour's Gordon Brown, and his special adviser Ed Balls, were on the same page, with the particular advantage that they were likely to be in a position to implement the policies. In spite of all the hard work and Margaret's great leadership, I do not recall anyone at a political level putting a Liberal Democrat stamp on the economic debate.

Of course, Labour had, for very good reasons, not outlined their determination to make the Bank independent, but it happened very quickly after their landslide victory.

My personal reaction to the 1997 election was complex. My own result was miserable. The Liberal Democrats were not in the position they needed to be. On the other hand, we had a new MP in Sittingbourne and Sheppey and in the run up to election day I had actually sent him an encouraging message. Above all, we had a new Government which, with a few reservations, I welcomed as a break from Tory domination.

The day after the election, I was driving through Maidstone and Blair was on the radio welcoming a new dawn and I found myself welling up with excitement and a sort of joy.

However, the Labour Manifesto had said,

'We are committed to a referendum on the voting system for the House of Commons. An Independent commission on voting systems will be appointed early to recommend a proportional alternative to first past the post'

The Commission was led by Roy Jenkins. No action was ever taken. Many Liberal Democrats felt betrayed but the cause had been lost in the Labour landslide and the caution of the Liberal Democrats in advance of the election.

The mould survived.

I did have a go at being selected as a Liberal Democrat candidate for the European parliament, a ballot in which a talented man called Chris Huhne came top. He went on to a successful career in Brussels and Westminster until 2013, when he resigned after being found guilty of perverting the course of justice over a driving ban. I was not helped by turning up at hustings around the south east and declaring that I was not in favour of the country joining the European single currency. That was about as astute as anyone turning up at a later UKIP meeting and arguing in favour.

One particularly heinous bit of self-inflicted harm during this pointless campaign was missing the chance to go to the Wembley 1998 play-off final between Charlton and Sunderland, probably the best match of its kind so far. The teams drew four-all and Charlton won on penalties and were promoted to the Premiership division.

Instead, I went down to Battle in Sussex to join the local Liberal Democrats in an exhilarating coffee morning.

For a period after that, in my own mind, I had done politics from an active point of view. I would stay interested but I resigned my membership of the Liberal Democrats, believing they were unlikely to raise their parliamentary ambitions in Kent. At this point, I did not think I would want to seek election again in local government.

It did not turn out like that.

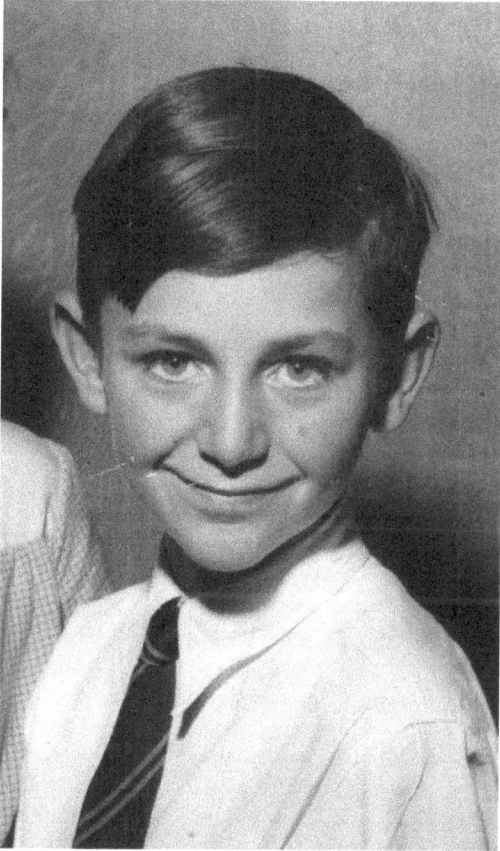

At Primary School 1956.
"Secure and self-confident."

Dartford 1st X1 1965.
"Meant a great deal to me."

29th March 1969 and marriage to Christine

On Alliance Girls High School campus at Kikuyu with Catherine

2002 with Tony Blair and Angela Harrison in No 10. "He gave the impression that what I had to say was really important."

2006 with Derek Wyatt MP, promoting the FA Cup and Charlton Athletic at our local primary school. (Photo by courtesy of the KM Group.)

My family 2014

May 2019. Swale's Rainbow Coalition.
Left to right Cllrs Monique Bonney (Independent),
Tim Valentine (Green Party), Me (Labour), Ben
Martin (Liberal Democrat) and Mike Baldock
(Swale Independent Alliance)
(Photo by courtesy of the KM Group.)

PART 3
1997-2023

8

NEW LABOUR

About two years into the Labour government, the local Labour MP, Derek Wyatt asked me up to his house in the village of Rodmersham. After an exploratory chat about the economy, he suggested I might like to be his local press officer. I would have to join the Labour Party but not necessarily get too embedded into local activities.

This was the beginning of our working together on a lot more than press releases. It indicated a generosity of spirit by both of us that two parliamentary opponents formed a team that was later described by the local press as formidable. We have stayed friends, even going together to Charlton Athletic fixtures.

Indeed, on one occasion, we both got kitted out in our respective Charlton shirts and took the FA Cup around some local schools.

Joining the Labour Party was manageable but I did have to consider how I felt about Blair as a Prime Minister. I admired the communication skills that had helped to deliver us from the Conservatives. I believed a range of Labour politicians could have won in 1997 but only Blair could have achieved such a stunning landslide. It suggested that Labour might be in office for a number of years, an opportunity that no previous Labour Prime Minister had enjoyed. But it was uncomfortable knowing that Tony Blair would not entirely break from the Thatcherite consensus. I expected New Labour to reverse the decline in public service investment of previous years but I was worried by the prospect of social market reforms of public services that would make key areas like health and education less accountable to public scrutiny and more market orientated in their ethos.

I found solace in the presence of Gordon Brown at the Treasury. When we held a press conference to announce my conversion, I was asked the inevitable question, how could I, a Liberal Democrat candidate two years before, support the Labour Party. I said Brown's decision to make the Bank of England independent in setting interest rates, his determination, then, to balance the current account budget and to find extra resources for investment in innovation and our neglected infrastructure were all consistent with the Liberal Democrat policies that I had had a very small part in agreeing. None of that was reported. Instead, there was talk of raised eyebrows at the astonishing fact that two election opponents were going to work together.

In subsequent years, the best of New Labour came from Gordon Brown, especially the injection of new funds into the NHS through a judicious increase in National Insurance contributions. I also thought, of course, that he and Ed Balls were right to set tests for entry into the single Euro currency, tests that in reality were not going to be met. Entry with its restrictive controls on fiscal and monetary policy were potentially too great a restraint on progressive UK economic policy.

My involvement with the Labour Party was not for long confined to writing press releases for Derek. In a fairly short space of time, I became the local party chairman, the campaign organiser and then a borough councillor once again, supposedly to provide a link for our MP. In 2002 I won in a ward with my good friend, and ex Liberal Democrat, Ghlin Whelan and we both stayed on the Council until this year.

As a key campaigner I was invited, along with many others, to drinks receptions at 10 Downing Street, hosted first by Tony Blair and then by Gordon Brown.

Blair worked the packed room with ease and charm, as did his wife and John Prescott, the latter in a more robust fashion. When Blair came round to talking to me, he gave the impression that what I had to say was important to him. That is a rare skill. Once the room had been thoroughly warmed, he stood on a stool and roused the room with wit and clarity and sent everyone home contented.

When Brown became Prime Minister, the reception was conducted in a different way. Instead of working the room, we were invited in pairs to go and shake his, and Sarah Brown's, hands in a formal way and without real conversation and when the speech came it was serious and stiffly delivered. The party did not last as long and there was less contentment as we key activists left Downing Street.

In electoral terms, Tony Blair was uniquely successful, winning three General Elections, two by landslides and the other comfortably. Harold Wilson also won four elections, though three very marginally and Margaret

Thatcher, like Blair, won three times with workable majorities. Most voters are not very interested in the details of politics but have a perception of whether someone is Prime Ministerial or not. I tend to think these three were accepted as Prime Ministers, if not always popular, because in their different ways they believed the role suited them and they were at ease with the psychological challenges of an isolated role. Many of our other post war Prime Ministers did not have that self-assurance. We now know, of course, that Boris Johnson was not well suited to a role where short-term political considerations and instant popularity need to be measured against the long term greater good. It hardly seems necessary to say that Liz Truss was as ill-suited to the role as anyone could be, and it is alarming to think that a majority of Conservative members ever thought she was. The current prime minister, at the time of writing, Rishi Sunak, is struggling to win public approval but the task of leading the party at this time seems a daunting one.

In the run-up to the 2001 election, I spent hours recording voter preferences, composing, and sending out mailshots, writing leaflets, organising delivery rounds, and mustering troops for canvas sessions. There were evenings when we had thirty door knockers on patrol and on election day, we had cohorts of 'knockers up' out on the stump. Labour was only six seats down on its landslide of 1997, despite a swing of 1.8% from Labour to the Conservatives, whilst the Labour vote was up in our seat by 5.2% and a swing against the national trend of 2.5% from Tory to Labour. It was the first time since 1966 that I had been able to vote for a winning candidate and the result was truly satisfying. The only qualification I would make is that when I went round canvassing, some people were adamantly Labour but not for reasons that I instantly associated with the values of the party, or anyone on the left. Was this the impact of Blair writing for the Daily Mail?

As I said, Ghlin and I won our Council seats in 2002 in our Chalkwell ward. Ghlin is a tireless campaigner and is open and friendly to voters. However, he sees no need for excessive diplomacy.

We were out canvassing together but on opposite sides of the road.

'Roger, this man doesn't want a leaflet'

'Tell him it's not for him but his wife and he has no right to decide whether she reads it or not'

Ghlin looking the man up and down,

'I doubt whether he has a wife'

The man, who might now be described by some as a 'gammon' was fairly non plussed.

When we joined the Labour group on the Council, we came under the leadership of Cllr Angela Harrison. Just as my now close working relationship with Derek was unusual, having been opposing candidates, my partnership with Angela was also interesting as she had been a fourteen-year-old pupil when I joined the teaching staff at Sheppey School in 1974. Whilst I did the campaign thinking for Derek's election campaigns in 2001 and 2005, Angela was his agent. For several years the three of us met every Friday in Angela's parlour in

Sheerness to eat fish and chips and to devise ways of linking the overall Labour message to local circumstances.

We never felt that the retention of this seat would be permanent and so there was a determination to deliver real gains for the community whilst we were there. Derek Wyatt was excellent at lobbying ministers and during his term of office, ministers high and low, visited the constituency. A community hospital on Sheppey was agreed by Frank Dobson but the cardinal objective was to secure a new crossing over the Swale channel that divides the Isle of Sheppey from the mainland of the constituency. The pressurising of ministers did not begin with Derek. I know my friend Tom Ledger as Liberal Democrat Leader of the Council had been to Westminster to talk to government ministers. However, the fact is that after three decades of talking about this essential project, the funding and delivery finally happened during the term of a Labour MP and a Labour government.

Some of us too, had spent many years arguing for a by-pass to be built to the North East of Sittingbourne, only to be told that it was impossible because funding would never be provided for a crossing over the Milton Creek. Derek spoke to John Prescott. The funding for the crossing emerged as did transport funding for the rest of the road, at least as far as the industrial estate on the north side of the town.

So, Labour had won two General Elections by landslides and this had resulted in our having a Labour MP in a constituency where the norm was Conservative domination at both local and parliamentary levels. We did not expect the next election, actually held in 2005, to be another landslide and we calculated that we would lose the seat without conducting an extraordinary campaign.

We kicked off the 2005 election campaign in January 2003. A team of canvassers went out every Thursday, aiming not at the strong Labour or Conservative wards, but those at the margins. We upped the frequency of leaflet deliveries, telephoning of voters, mailshots, and Derek's media profile.

Inevitably, the war in Iraq, began to have an impact but not always predictably. I remember one man telling me he had never voted Labour before, but he would now 'as long as Blair was Leader,' because he had supported the Americans in Iraq.

Our energetic campaigning showed up in party data and whilst we were probably regarded as expendable in the pursuit of another term of office, we were given extensive support in our attempts to save the seat.

As the election approached in 2005, we were given a clever young staff officer, Tim Waters, to help with our data use and planning. We had high profile visits from Jack Straw, John Prescott, and others, including Patricia Hewitt landing by helicopter on Tom Ledger's farm in Newington for one hour's canvassing in the village. We also had Mo Mowlam and Cherie Blair around one morning but for reasons above my pay grade to understand, we had to avoid them meeting each other. This involved a bit of subterfuge, which meant I had to substitute for Derek at a meeting with Age Concern. Mo and I entertained a room full of elderly members for over an hour. The Conservatives issued a press release saying that Age Concern were insulted by the substitution of their local MP by a mere member of staff, but I knew a lot of the members and they assured me later that they enjoyed our visit much more than those from other parties, who failed to engage in the same way.

The prized visit was by Gordon Brown. This was one where we anticipated the best media coverage and the television cameras were there.

We went to the Sure Start Centre in Sheerness, something that Labour was proud of and especially Brown himself. On this occasion Gordon Brown was totally relaxed and established good relationships immediately with the young parents. He got down on his knees and played with the children and was so obviously happy that we found it hard to get him out to do the necessary TV interviews.

Over the previous two years, Derek's time and energy had been much consumed with supporting employees at the Allied Wire and Steelworks in Sheerness. They were extremely anxious about the fate of their pensions following the closure of the company. Derek and Kevin Brennan, a Labour MP from Cardiff, were in the forefront of campaigning for a compensatory scheme backed by Government.

As it happened, Derek's contacts had been as much with the managers, as with the shopfloor workers and they had every reason to be appreciative of the effort he had put in on their behalf.

It was therefore not a welcome sight when the managers deliberately gate crashed our Sure Start event with protest banners. This was likely to have a material impact on Derek's re-election and his opportunity to continue to fight for them.

Naturally, the TV reporters saw this incursion as a bigger story than Brown's empathy with the Sure Start children, so I made sure that they could not easily get their cameras into the entrance space to record any confrontation but the protestors still made it on to the regional news bulletins.

I thought they were shabby. In 2007, they received 90% of their pensions at a cost to the government of £2.9 billion. They took this to be their right and reward for their campaigning. They never acknowledged the support they had from Derek and Kevin, without whom, in my opinion, they would have got nowhere.

The day before election day in 2005, we were out canvassing on the south side of Sittingbourne. Derek got a call from Martha Carney at the BBC saying they had crunched the numbers and concluded that we were going to lose. As usual, he took it phlegmatically. Later in the day, I was contacted by Rory Cellan Jones, also of the BBC, who said he was going to be the duty reporter at the count. I told him I still expected Derek to hold the seat by about 1000.

I was seriously wrong as Mr Cellan Jones was kind enough to let me know. The count showed that it was ridiculously close and when the Returning Officer gathered round the candidates and agents, he said that the Conservative candidate Gordon Henderson had won by

120 votes. I took it that that was final. Derek and his wife sat down calmly and began thinking about their future. Angela our agent was not so resigned.

She asked for a recount and was told she could not have one but as a sop we were offered a check on the stacks of votes. Almost immediately a Labour Councillor Jennie Ronan came up to me and said she had seen 50 votes for Wyatt in a Henderson pile. Further examination found more Wyatt votes misappropriated in both the Conservative pile and in that of the Liberal Democrats.

It was not long before the Returning Officer was again gathering round the principal players, but this time to report that Derek had won by 79 votes.

I assumed there would then have to be a total recount but there was not. It was not a victory that I felt particularly like celebrating. I was uneasy about the count. The fact that a recount was not allowed and that bundles of votes had been originally been put in the wrong piles suggested that there was a bit too much haste in a contest that was bound to be very close.

However, we had won.

The fact that we had bucked expectations owed much to the strength of our campaigning, the high-profile support given by the central party and the personal votes that Derek had earned over the previous eight years. A lot of these personal votes are won by an MP's office staff and the hard work they do on individual issues. Derek owed much to   Joy Grice, Kelly Williams and Amanda Vanderstraaten in his local office and Anna Yallop and Jenny Sheridan in Westminster.

Before the election of 2005, Christine and I had our own personal lives to get on with. We made several visits to Paris to see Catherine, who lived and worked there for several years. She taught English as a Foreign Language, sometimes to high powered Executives in the finance district. She did some teaching at the Sorbonne and had some interesting academic friends. We visited the Quai D'Orsay, the Galerie Lafayette and Montmartre most regularly.

In November 2004 we spent a week in Chicago, sharing Richard's apartment during a short stay of work that he was doing there. We felt sublimely relaxed in the stunning architecture of the city, went out to the suburbs in search of Frank Lloyd Wright, enjoyed the Chicago Art Gallery and lazed around Grant Park on the shores of Lake Michigan.

One evening the three of us booked to go to the Chicago Opera to see *Aida*. We ordered a taxi and asked to go to the Opera but probably pronounced it a bit like Oppra. The driver said he did not realise Oprah Winfrey was in town and was disappointed when we put him right.

It was general election time in the United States. We went shopping on election day and a shop assistant urged us to go and vote for John Kerry, the Democrat Presidential candidate. We said we would if we could but we did not have the vote. She said it was no matter because everyone she knew was voting Democrat and so success was assured. Of course, Chicago is not typical of the whole country.

On the previous days, we had been fascinated but alarmed by the political adverts in support of candidates;

not just the Presidential candidates but senatorial, gubernatorial, and state legislature and other civic candidates. The more local the elections were, the more personal and vituperative the ads became with one female candidate being constantly derided because of where she lived. As the ad voice over kept repeating, 'She just doesn't care.'

Voters in Illinois were also voting for a Federal Senator. The Democrat candidate won by a massive landslide. His name was Barack Obama and four years later he was back in Grant Park for his Presidential victory speech.

Through this decade too, we were making longish domestic trips to see John. He spent three years at Durham University (on the Stockton campus) and then four years at Exeter.

These years were lived not just in the glow of a Labour Government but also with Charlton Athletic in the Premier football league. I knew at the time it would not last, in either case, but for Charlton these seven years were the best of the nearly seventy years I have been a supporter. Because for the most part, they were a decent side at this level, with international players and able to win both home and away to such 'big' clubs as Arsenal, Liverpool, Chelsea, Tottenham, and Manchester City. They never beat Manchester United. Now in 2023 they continue to struggle in what is realistically division three.

John was a regular supporter and in March 2004 it was decided that if I went to see him and took an empty suitcase, to bring home his washing, we could go and see Newcastle and Charlton. The understanding was that after depositing the suitcase, we would go on to St James

Park. I caught a train from King's Cross in plenty of time, along with many other Charlton supporters, who intended to get to Newcastle early in the afternoon for the half past five kick off. We got as far as Peterborough and then the train kept stopping and then going on very slowly.

It was the wind.

The journey took hours and John got himself to Newcastle station and we finally arrived by half time. We ran up to the ground but all the turnstile entrances were locked. I banged furiously on a door and a kindly steward arrived. I told him how far I had travelled, why we were late and, notwithstanding I was carrying a suitcase at a time of some security sensitivity, he ushered us in. And up to the Directors suite. There we were given a 'hullo fellers' from Peter Beardsley and sat down in two spare seats, set aside for us.

Newcastle was two-nil in the lead at half time. Despite that the second half was worth watching. Charlton dominated. Jensen scored and just as they seemed likely to equalise, Shearer elicited a penalty from the referee.

Shearer had also scored the first goal and Jermaine Jenas the second

We caught the train packed with home fans back to Stockton, stopping at Sunderland and Hartlepool. We avoided saying anything to identify ourselves with Charlton. Once off the train, I was asked whether I was disappointed at missing half the game. I was not at all. It had been quite an adventure and I still had the empty suitcase to fill in his house.

By the end of 2004, Christine and I were both 60 years old. We determined that we should now take the opportunity to take more holidays and I resolved that it was about time our priorities were much more Christine's priorities, though I doubt whether this resolution has since been fully realised. But it is there as a sort of paradigm.

In September 2006, we went to New England to enjoy the fall. We flew to Boston via Washington. When we touched down in Washington, they said not to worry but we were leaking oil on to the runway. By the time we finally got off the plane and gone through their extremely cautious immigration checks, we had missed the flight to Boston. We waited for about six hours and when we got to Boston at midnight, they said they did not have our luggage. It did eventually arrive, and we went on a tour through Massachusetts, New Hampshire, Vermont, and Maine. We then spent another week in Boston and drove round to Cape Cod. We stopped at Hyennas and sat on a deserted beach. A man eventually walked by and we asked if we could get a drink in the large hotel over to our right,

'Don't reckon so, that's the Kennedy's house.'

We also drove up to Exeter in New Hampshire, where I had spent a happy term of teaching practice at the Phillips Academy nearly forty years before. It had been a boys' only school in 1967 but now it was co-educational and a very charming girl updated us a little on life there now.

When Derek Wyatt got re-elected to parliament in 2005, Angela Harrison and I won seats, for the first time, on Kent County Council. Holding these elections on the same day as a general election that still returned seven Labour MPs in Kent boosted our representation on the county council. It was, as ever, overwhelmingly Conservative but we had twenty-one seats and were recognised formally as the opposition.

This entitled us to official shadow cabinet posts and I was elected as spokesman on education. I found that a stimulating role, notwithstanding the lack of real authority.

The first time I spoke in full council, it was to oppose a Labour Government policy, which the ruling Conservatives found intriguing . As part of the reform of public services the government were proposing to introduce trust schools that would be able to run independently of local authorities. It was another manifestation of what had been grant maintained status or now academies and it is inspired by the social market philosophy that public sector institutions will be more efficient if they pursue their particular interests rather than the interests of a wider service.

The Conservatives agreed with me but only because they were reluctant to see a weakening of their control of Kent education. A meeting had been arranged with a junior education minister called Jacqui Smith. I was deputed to attend on behalf of Kent County Council and vigorously made the case against the trust idea. She was very stubborn and kept repeating the prepared justification that it would make schools 'free' , able to innovate, be enterprising and more efficient. Happily, the policy was abandoned by the government in 2007. It was strongly opposed by head teachers and in cabinet by Ed Miliband.

Considerable time was also taken up with a related issue. The Labour Government was prepared to allow obviously failing schools to be taken over by Academy Trusts. This was a touch of social market intervention for a straitened minority, and one obvious candidate was the Sheppey School in our constituency. This was where I had taught in the 1970s, where I and many others had invested much hope and energy but which had declined in the process of trying to reverse its progressive agenda.

Kent County Council had a proactive Director of Education at this time. His name was Graham Badman and he wanted to get the government to invest millions of pounds in Sheppey and also, in so doing, to end the three-tier system on the Island, which he believed held back young people; that was a system where children went to First School from 5-9, Middle School form 9-13 and Upper School from 13-18.

He wanted Derek Wyatt's backing and I was possibly a useful link.

It was explained to me that this would be the only way to get the investment that Sheppey education needed and reluctantly I agreed to support the idea. I think this might be called a pragmatic decision.

It was said that the Sheppey Academy would have unique virtues. As the local authority was a part sponsor, it would retain a special interest. The school would be in the vanguard in adopting new vocational courses and qualifications and in addition it would have a close working relationship with Dulwich College, who would offer talented students opportunities for academic and sporting tuition.

We were all invited to a brainstorming meeting at Dulwich College, chaired by Andrew Adonis, like me an ex Liberal Democrat, but by this time a Labour Government minister. His enthusiasm for this project seemed unbridled. Dulwich College was represented by one of its governors, Andrew Turnbull, who had been Head of the Civil Service until 2005 and, it seemed to me, later stayed loyal to the project longer than most.

The Academy did eventually materialise. Until recently it has been run by the Oasis Academy Trust but they are to be replaced by another Trust in the dubious hope that a proprietorial change will solve fundamental problems.

The county council has no locus standi. The school is split into two sites and it does not work. There is no Dulwich College involvement. Vocational options on a grand scale have not been delivered. There is still a great exodus of secondary school children to all schools in Sittingbourne, selective and secondary moderns. The intake of pupils is well below prescribed numbers. The results are disheartening and teacher recruitment parlous.

Providing Sheppey with a sound system of Secondary education is still a cardinal local priority. Young people there are disadvantaged and economic investment is choked out by a skills shortage. It is a sad situation.

On Saturday October 6th 2007, Derek and I went to the Valley. Charlton were no longer in the top division and drew with Barnsley one-all in a typically uninspiring game. Throughout the match we talked of more urgent matters. We believed that we would have to be campaigning for a general election from Monday morning.

I said I understood our regional office would be sending out leaflets so that we could as ever 'hit the ground running.' I would organise deliveries and martial up some canvass teams. We would issue an immediate optimistic press release, though in reality we had to be prepared for a loss of the seat.

As we walked back to our car, Derek, who rarely strayed from his phone, suddenly exclaimed

'It is off. There is not going to be a General Election'

I was shocked and felt an immediate sense of foreboding.

It may have been that Gordon Brown only regarded an election as an option but the speculation had gone too far, and his apparently late withdrawal caused permanent damage to him and to the Labour Party.

It is said that favourable polls for the Tories in marginal seats had swayed the decision. The polls may have been influenced by commitments made at the Conservative Conference about inheritance tax. Such movements are often very transitory. Brown would probably have defeated Cameron in a general election even if with a reduced majority.

In all humanity, it is easy to understand Brown's reticence. After waiting so long to be Prime Minister how could he throw it away after a few months? Somehow, the Labour Party had erred by letting the speculation grow.

I have no doubt that this date, October 6, was a fateful one for Labour, but possibly for British politics in general.

Nobody in 2007 predicted the economic and financial crash here and around the world that followed from irresponsible mortgage sales in the United States. But the financial crisis of 2008-2009 still has an impact on international and UK politics in a most destructive way.

Had the 2007 general election actually happened and Labour had won, our country could have been steered through the recession with regeneration rather than austerity as the preferred approach. Alternatively, had Cameron's Tories come to office, then they would have taken the hit for the recession of 2008-2009. In either case, Labour could well have won the 2012 election and our politics might have been very different over the last decade.

It is a plausible scenario.

My wife, Christine, has always been very supportive in my political activities, notwithstanding the impact it can have on family life. During the time that Derek was MP, she was also very supportive of him too and he responded by, for example, reserving a place for her in the Queen's gallery at the state opening of parliament.

When we heard that the Prime Minister's wife, Sarah, would be joining us in Sittingbourne for a visit to our Milton children's centre, Derek invited Christine to join the official party. Meanwhile, I stayed at home and prepared tea for our guest and members of the local party.

Mrs Brown was very keen to talk to local members. Ghlin Whelan scarcely moved a foot away from her and later declared that 'she was lovely.' She assured us all that Gordon would stem the drift away from Labour.

Sadly, however, and in spite of the way he and Alastair Darling managed the financial crisis, the pressure on his leadership continued.

A pleasant political reporter from the *Times* rang me. She has worked more recently for *Channel 4* in a variety of key roles. She asked if she could come to our constituency to talk to members about the Labour leadership. I replied that I had a group of twelve members attending an all-day campaign session in Sheerness and that she was most welcome to spend the day with us.

Which she did, and I had to admire the effort she put in to fulfil the story that her editor had sent her to file.

I picked her up from Sittingbourne station and tried to brief her on the local constituency. I said it was very marginal, with some wards being strongly Conservative and some Labour.

She asked me,

'What is a ward?"

Clearly Times political correspondents did not need a granular awareness of constituency politics.

Throughout the day, our members were asked in so many different ways whether they would like Brown to stand down. None would oblige.

By lunchtime I suggested she go out into the High Street and ask some voters. She came back a little forlorn.

'Many of them are still with Labour and they all want

Brown to stay.'

I later took her to Sittingbourne High Street where she found no further joy.

When I dropped her at the station, I said I looked forward to the article saying that Brown should stay.

It never appeared.

I also got a call one evening from a researcher from *BBC Newsnight*. As Chairman of the local party, I was asked

'Do you think the Labour Party should replace Gordon Brown as Leader?'

'No'

'But if they did, who do you think should succeed him?'

'I haven't considered that and neither has my local party'

'But can I ask you to think about it? Who do you think would be the best person?'

'Me' I suggested and the interview ended.

Who knows? If David Miliband, the intended answer, had become leader politics might have shaped out differently too.

By 2009, the political atmosphere in this country was toxic. The local Conservatives were making a load of unpleasant comments about Derek's personal life. They were inappropriate and insensitive and we went to see the editor and senior reporter of our local newspapers, the East Kent and Sheppey Gazettes. We explained why the opposition comments were insensitive and they very fairly agreed to edit them out of future copy.

So, when Derek decided not to stand in the 2010 election, we gave the news to them as an exclusive. They published on a Wednesday morning. I went off to Beckenham with John to watch cricket but it was not long before I was getting aggressive phone calls from other media. Why asked the rival local paper group, the Kent Messenger, had we not shared the news with them and I struggled for an answer. Then Regional BBC television rang from Tunbridge Wells. They could not find Derek so would I go down to Tunbridge Wells to do an interview.

'I'm sorry I'm in Beckenham enjoying a day out with my son.'

'But couldn't you find time to drive to Tunbridge Wells?'

'Not really, we got here by train. Why don't you come here and I will do an interview at the cricket ground?

They could not do that of course. Instead, they found a rather supercilious political journalist from a distinctly unfriendly national newspaper to say something dismissive about Derek, so our decision to reward the Gazette slightly backfired.

9

THE FAILURE OF
CONTEMPORARY POLITICS

I started this chapter with the clear intention of demonstrating that after 2010 I was less focussed on our politics, with more time for personal life and for those who deserve my attention.

Thus, it starts. But my political focus did not really diminish after 2010.

This chapter evolves as a comment on the state of politics, my frustration and disappointment, in fact anger, with what can only be described as the failure of contemporary politics.

The general election on May 6 marked the end of thirteen years of Labour government. In Sittingbourne and Sheppey, it also meant we no longer had a Labour MP. On a more trivial level, it was almost the end of my time as a councillor as I scraped home by thirty votes from a Conservative young lady called Emma Bridges in the Swale Council elections held on the same day.

There was to be no more going down to the constituency office to crunch electoral detail, to give advice on casework, to discuss tactics or to write supportive press releases or pamphlets.

Now was the time for other things; to give more time to the things Christine wanted to do, to the family, to a bit of relaxation. Well, that, as I said, was the good intention. In reality these last thirteen years , notwithstanding a passing visit to India and Australia, have seen me more pre-occupied by politics than I could have imagined. Always on the point of giving up, I became more and more activated.

This chapter is mainly a plaintive commentary on our sad contemporary politics , and the final chapter is an update on my own personal political story which ended with something of a surprise.

But to begin with, we most deliberately resumed our joint determination to travel a lot more. And we have done so, with visits to France predominating: to Paris, Normandy, the Loire Valley, the Dordogne, Savoy, Provence, Annecy, Languedoc, and the Riviera. But we have also been to Spain, to Seville, Granada, and Barcelona, and we have made many more trips around the United Kingdom.

However, having lived in Africa and visited both the United States and South America, our plan was to organise two overseas trips to somewhere new.

We settled on Australia and India. This was by mutual consent but I had personal reasons for these choices.

My dad had spent quite a lot of his time when I was a small child in Australia and it had a kind of familiarity. I knew the enormous significance of the Melbourne Cup.

Since 1954, I had followed test cricket from grounds like Sydney and Melbourne. Our son Richard had spent a year there after graduating and a number of friends pressed us to go.

Of India, I had always had an interest. At school the E.M. Forster novel *A Passage to India* had had quite an impact on my outlook. As a child and adolescent, I had regularly listened to the radio programme *From our Own Correspondent* and my favourite reporter was always Mark Tully in Delhi, with his deep love of the country and his understanding of the people's spiritual roots. I knew something of the history of British India and followed, in a pretty superficial way their post-colonial politics. In my student days I had talked romantically about going to live and work in India, but I never did .

These were my reasons for prioritising these two adventures, because for us they were adventures, notwithstanding that many people we knew almost regarded them as a matter of routine.

It was to be Australia first. We organised a month at the end of 2011 and into 2012, involving stays in Melbourne and Sydney, a stop off in Singapore, an excursion down the Ocean Road, and visits into the wine fields of New South Wales. And we had tickets for the Ashes Tests in Melbourne and Sydney.

About a month before we were due to set off, I went to pick Christine up from our local station. I had a quick chat with Gordon Henderson, who had been elected as the Conservative MP in 2010 and then I started to see a cascade of black spots in my right eye. Within a few days, I had been operated on and sent home to sit bolt upright in an armchair for the next four weeks.

There was to be no Australia. I could not even watch the cricket on TV. Instead, we played some mournful tapes about some of the horrors of the Spanish Civil War and I did listen to commentaries of the Boxing Day test from the MCG (Melbourne Cricket Ground). We thought that was that for Australia.

I needed a further operation on my eye but by early 2013 we could travel and booked a package tour to India. This was scarcely what I had thought of doing as a student but it was good enough for us now. It is a very familiar tour, around a triangle from Delhi to Agra and then Jaipur. After that we took a long train journey to Simla.

Of course, we visited only the most famous sites; the Gandhi Memorial Garden in Delhi, the Taj Mahal in Agra, the Mughal Amber Fort in Jaipur and finally Government House in Simla, where Mountbatten and Nehru stitched up the partition of India.

We travelled in a comfort zone, stayed in luxurious hotels, and mixed jovially with our tour party. Our Indian guide was good. On the long coach trips around this triangle, he told us a great deal about Indian history and culture, religion, politics and where he saw India in the modern world. He was an informative and solicitous guide but I think he was inclined to think that some tourists were on a jolly and not truly interested in his country. After one very erudite talk on the way from Agra to Jaipur he asked for questions and laughed with something not far short of contempt when the bulk of the enquiries were about litter.

In 2016, my youngest son John married Hannah in Tuscany. They are a very thoughtful couple and surprised us by suggesting the following year that we could join them and re-visit the aborted tour of 2011. We would therefore stop at Singapore, do two test matches in Melbourne and Sydney, do the Ocean Road and the wine tour, not to mention a night sitting out watching for the arrival of penguins. They did all the arranging with quite astonishing elan. It was the best of times. I felt physically and emotionally moved going into the two test grounds. The food was exceptionally good. Amongst many wonderful dinners was one in a fish restaurant in Warrnambool, looking out to sea and knowing the only land to the south was the Antarctic.

The two cities are endearing in many ways. They are supposed to be serious rivals and that was evidenced on New Year's Eve, when Melbourne sought to rival Sydney for celebratory noise that almost reached thermonuclear proportions.

The short stay in Singapore was very interesting. It is remarkable the way that Lee Kwan Yew took Singapore out of the Malaysian Federation, created unity out of potential chaos with a brand of nationalist puritan socialism and then on the foundations of which the island has become a centre of world capitalism. For many, there will be wariness about the uniform authoritarianism, but no visitors complain of excessive litter.

I returned from Australia with a greater fondness than before. At some levels, there appears to be an enduring link to our own country. Some television news contained surprisingly many packages from the BBC with a striking interest in events at home. I picked up one popular newspaper containing a review of the *Netflix series the Crown*. The reviewer of obviously conservative inclinations was most affronted by the portrayal of Harold McMillan as a devious politician in the 1950s, suggesting perhaps that her emotions were stronger than her knowledge of that period.

But Australia has changed radically from the 1950s. It is a complex multi-ethnic country with strong cultural and economic ties to Asia as much as to our country. We celebrated Christmas in the Anglican Cathedral in Melbourne, where services are conducted for English speaking Christians but also for people from Indonesia.

In the wine lands of New South Wales, they stressed how important the China market was to them and other sectors of the economy look to Japan and Korea. Individuals I spoke to were anxious about the election of Trump to the American Presidency, fearing the impact on their region of his erratic approach to China. I also felt that the country as a whole was much more interested in trade agreements with the European Union than with the United Kingdom, notwithstanding the deal quite recently trumpeted by our government, a deal that is very much in the interest, of course, of Australian beef producers rather than our own farmers.

There is also a high level of social responsibility observed at least in the cities of Australia. There are continuously reinforced messages, broadcast on public transport and on scoreboards on cricket grounds and they are principally around taking the risks from exposure from the sun very seriously, being very conscious of safety on the roads and above all, showing respect for others, regardless of race, class, or gender.

On climate matters, it is devastating to see the impact on Australia, the droughts, the fires and then the floods. It is sad and it should be a vivid reminder to us of how serious the climate emergency really is and a powerful nudge to those who want to minimise it for self- centred short-term reasons. Happily, the Australians last year voted out their right-wing populist global warming denier in an election where the climate was the major issue.

The climate emergency is only one of the global crises facing the whole of humanity. We now know that the regular warnings about the spread of pandemics should have been heeded. We need too, to recognise the threats posed by enduring inequality around the world, with mass migrations in search of survival and a better life helping to stimulate a brand of right-wing populism. As in Australia the choking impact of populist ideology may be abating, with the rejection of Morrison being preceded by the defeats of Trump, Le Pen and Bolsonaro. There is still a long way to go. The rabid right is a real danger in the United Kingdom and in Europe.

The condition of our global and domestic politics over the last decade has been profoundly depressing. Where we need leaders of intellectual and ethical integrity, with vision and an international perspective to tackle our existential problems, we have instead, with few exceptions, leaders stunningly ill-suited to meet these challenges. It makes little difference whether or not countries claim to be democratic.

Nothing illustrates the decline of world governance more

vividly than the disaster that was the American Presidency between 2016 and 2020. Trump disrupted world diplomacy, trade and environmental agreements and tainted democracy in his own country, campaigning through hate and stunning misinformation. It was a glad day when he was beaten by President Biden but his malevolence continues to have strong roots in the United States and will warp politics there for some time to come. There has always been an extreme right in America, and conspiracy theorists like the John Birch Society. It is perverse how the notion of freedom is weaponised to justify extreme nationalism, white supremacy, and insurrection. As the Unite the Right rally of 2016 showed, the various intimidating groups can be drawn together through social media but what is so alarming is that the Trump Presidency and its aftermath has emboldened these dangerous people, a threat to the freedom they falsely espouse.

As elsewhere, the political culture has also drastically declined in our own country in the last decade.

No-one would seriously pretend that there was an ideal past of exclusively rational policy making, of electors weighing up their wishes through the analysis of real evidence, or of them being able to select leaders of impeccable sense and integrity.

However, we have moved radically away from any semblance of that ideal. Over recent years the prevalent influences on voters are emotional, identity rather than policy, group alienation and hostility, and false and misleading slogans that seek to exclude expertise and real experience.

This depressing climate has brought to prominence people of dubious merit, promoted by a political media easily attracted to outrageous opinions in preference to measured and informed comment. It is not only some unlikely politicians who have benefited from this culture but many who are described as journalists. There are a number of individuals in the media who, in some cases possibly against their own instincts, have chosen to believe they can earn a lot more than otherwise, by being offensive and irrational, by stirring up emotions and stoking narrow sectional feelings. And it is not surprising because they get the media attention they crave; their notoriety increases and it earns them lucrative appearances in press and television.

There is a lot of ostentatious patriotism in our political culture, with politicians of all colours feeling it imperative to use the union flag as a campaign prop .

We are patriotic and we should be but what we should be proud of is our tolerance, our openness, and the fact that we have always welcomed those fleeing from war, like the Belgians in 1914

We should be proud too of our stable democracy but that is harder to be when our politics descends into toxicity and extremely partisan decision making.

What is not patriotic is xenophobic attitudes to people from other countries or to international institutions which this country has previously supported in order to create a better world.

The climate over recent years has pushed our political spectrum to the right. It is sometimes dignified at an ideological level as libertarianism, a collective passion for pushing back the leviathan of the state and granting to individuals unlimited power to make personal decisions, regardless of wider social responsibilities and the need to tackle our real problems in a cohesive way.

We saw some of this articulated at extreme levels during the height of the Covid pandemic, with protests against doing those things that we mostly recognise as necessary for the safety of us all.

There has been a mythological trend emerging that says all the measures adopted to get us through the pandemic crisis were unnecessary.

This is perverse, because what the pandemic really underlined was our responsibility to each other, to stay safe to keep everyone safe, and the dependence we all have on government intervention in a critical episode. This transparent truth has now been further enhanced by the intervention that government has been forced into by the energy and cost of living crisis. If as a patriotic country we wish to keep everyone safe, then smaller government is not the way forward. Smaller government is the ideological drive of those who feel that our overall cake is diminishing and their aim is to preserve as much of the cake as possible for those already well provided for.

The libertarian right has taken a strong hold over sections of the Conservative Party, restricting the freedom of recent prime ministers to take balanced decisions in the country's interest.

During the premiership of David Cameron, I was

privileged to be invited to a private discussion group at Westminster, including both Tory and Labour MPs and outside commentators. One of the latter asked the question whether Cameron was our worst prime minister ever. There was general agreement that this was not an outlandish question but the reality is that since Cameron we have had to continually re-assess our criteria of what the worst prime minister might be. Because to follow Cameron, we have the stubborn inflexibility of May, the mendacity and incompetence of Johnson and the idiotic fixations of Truss. The current incumbent simply has to struggle with the chaos, to which he has contributed, and the impossible disunity in his governing party.

Apart from the transparent shortcomings of Tory leadership since 2010, I have become indebted for my understanding of the politicians involved by a series of books on their lives at 10 Downing Street by Anthony Seldon, who has a not totally unsympathetic understanding of the Conservative party. What emerges from these books is not just the personality shortcomings but a clear understanding that all three were simply not very good at the job. Behind the scenes, we get a picture of in some cases laziness, of inability to inspire, to make decisions, to be genuinely collegiate or to ultimately trust their own judgement.

Under all of them the Conservative Party has become increasingly divisive and far too impressed by its right wing or by right wing pressures from outside their party.

Traditional Conservatism which cherished our institutions, such as the judiciary, has been marginalised by the populist right, which often plays at being anti-establishment and anti-elite. It is a charade but it has left social democrats to act as protectors of our institutions. It is leaving moderate traditional liberal Conservatives with no place to go, at least for the time being.

The home-grown populist zeitgeist has been hard on the centre and centre left. It has been hard for the Labour Party, a party whose stance on social equality, internationalism and the need for a benign interventionist state has so often been derided. The long and tiresome concentration on the issue of the United Kingdom leaving the European Union presented Labour with challenges that were not solved because they could not be solved.

What of the campaign to leave the European Union? It succeeded by injecting into our politics a degree of toxicity, disingenuity and delusion that has left scars and an absence of focus on genuine issues. The drive came from the economic right and it was motivated by a strong impulse to leave the social democratic economic model of the European Union, where markets worked within a regulatory framework to protect workers, the environment, and the consumer, to a more American style economy, in which many of the movers had financial interests. That is why leaving the EU per se, the Council of Ministers, the Commission, or the Parliament, was never enough and why May's attempts to retain links with the single market were doomed, as long as the right had control of the Conservative party.

The leave campaign was aided by incoherence on the Labour side, with a leadership equally uncomfortable with the single market, for very different ideological reasons, a party membership in favour of remaining, but a Labour voting electorate drawn into the emotionalism of the leave campaigners.

It is said that the result of the Referendum in 2016 came as a total surprise to Cameron and Osborne, but it appears as though it shocked the leavers too, with Johnson exclaiming with customary expletives that there was no plan to follow.

But it should not have been such a surprise. This country had always been semi-detached. Governments such as those of Thatcher and Blair, had whilst securing a stronger link between the United Kingdom and the European Community, used sceptical rhetoric to keep the right wing media at bay. Coverage was nearly always negative and the growing economic importance of the European market, after Thatcher had signed the Single Act in 1986, was never explained. As I have said above, the motivation behind the Leave Campaign was to change our economic model and it is now the difficulties with that which leads some Leavers to moan that their project has failed. Immigration, of course, was used as a weapon and false promises were made about health service spending. Failure on these fronts has changed the public mood.

Meanwhile, though not every thing in the economy is adversely affected, some key parts are: agriculture, manufacturing especially of cars, finance, care, hospitality, tourism, and pharmaceuticals are just some examples, whilst we have some trade deals that are less advantageous than the European ones, we previously had access to.

Meanwhile Labour's woes of the last decade were not just circumstantial. We did not help ourselves.

Whilst the inevitable ambivalence over leaving the European Union left a legacy that in 2019 drew many voters away from the party, we have been afflicted too, by the enduring perception that Labour was responsible for the financial crisis of 2009. Just as the current government had to use fiscal measures to meet the Covid pandemic and the energy cost crises, so Brown and Darling had to do so in 2009. In the years that followed the coalition government of Cameron and Clegg successfully managed to flip the cure for the crisis as the cause of the crisis, and, with considerable media support, assigned all economic consequences to the 'mess left by Labour'. Both coalition parties were peculiarly ill qualified to make this charge, as Cameron had endorsed Labour spending plans in 2008 and Clegg had complained that the fiscal stimulus was too modest to aid recovery. Perhaps the only legitimate critic was the Liberal Democrat spokesman, Vince Cable, who had suggested that Brown was over keen to liberalise the financial markets, but of course, liberalising the financial markets was the position of Cameron and the Conservatives. Well, that is politics.

My disappointment was that the Leadership of the Labour Party in the period between 2010 and 2015 did little, or nothing to push back on the Labour mess smear and it became an inevitable part of political discourse in the minds of the electorate. Indeed, it seemed at times, during this period, that leading Labour members, who owed so much to Brown, were ready ignobly to accept the smear.

What was equally disappointing was the way in which public finance deficits were equated with overall economic competence. So, whilst the Tory/Lib Dem coalition relied on austerity in public services and a general lack of an industrial strategy to leave us with low productivity and poor investment, Labour was regarded as less competent because we had left a borrowing deficit. As I have said, this was a financial necessity in 2009, just as it was a necessity in 2020 and 2022 to borrow. We shall see how far the Conservatives are going to be stigmatised in the years ahead. Labour may win again, but it will need to address the electorate's carefully moulded view of our economic competence. This is what Rachel Reeves is endeavouring to do, but she will not want to lose core Labour supporters on the way.

Our economy is now in a pedestrian state, partly due to global forces, but also because the long years of Conservative austerity has turned us into a low productivity, low growth economy. The genuine difficulties the current Government must face were intensified to an alarming extent by the mindless attempt to go for growth in September 2022 during the flawed premiership of Truss.

The notion that growth would come from unfunded tax cuts, without any fiscal plan, owed something to the same ideology that connived at the exit from the single market in Europe, that it would create new opportunities. It has not, it will not and we could do with hearing a lot less from these ideological sources. Proper growth can only come from investment, in technology, in skills and in infrastructure not from ideological gobbledegook.

But to return to Labour travails. Some of those in the leadership of the Labour Party during the coalition years between 2010 and 2015 just did not seem to grasp the fundamentals of opposition. A glaring example was the coalition 'Reform of the NHS.'

Having stoutly promised no further top-down reorganisation and with the Prime Minister Cameron barely grasping the rationale for reform, a divided government was open to forensic scrutiny by the opposition. That meant detailed and expert analysis of the failings of the bill in conjunction with health professionals, not just rehearsing predictable slogans about not trusting the Tories with the NHS. The most sustained analysis came from Liberal Democrat, Shirley Williams, in the House of Lords but she eventually gave in and we got what were unpopular changes to the Health Service.

Cameron's Coalition government generated many fertile opportunities for a strong opposition in the period between 2011 and 2014. It was led by a Prime Minister with a tendency towards indolent and ill prepared decision-making. He fumbled his way through constitutional change in Scotland and Europe and left the door open for UKIP. His Chancellor of the Exchequer produced a derided omnishambles budget and failed to reach his deficit targets, the very pretext for austerity. There were troubles in foreign policy, over Syria for example, and on education, Gove was given licence to pursue reforms that were manifestly ill conceived and unwelcome to teachers and educationists and of little help to our youngsters. Without any evidence, it was supposed that turning all schools into academies would raise standards for all children. Standards generally meant imposing expectations on children to benefit from a 1950s style grammar school education, a process that does not improve outcomes but guarantees that more youngsters fail.

But, as with health reform, the opposition from the Labour party at Westminster was largely void. During the period of troubles experienced by the Tory led coalition, there seemed to me to be an absence of coherent and collective opposition from the Labour front bench.

Which brings me to the other manifest problem since 2010, our party leadership. Whilst I did not vote for either Ed Miliband as Leader in 2010, nor Jeremy Corbyn in 2015, I have no axe to grind, as so many have in our party. However, what I can report is my own personal experience of canvassing for Labour during the 2010-2019 period and the response I got on the doorstep to these two leaders.

In a constituency like Sittingbourne and Sheppey, and many like it outside the large Metropolitan areas, there is not much room for doubts about our Leadership if we are to win.

The doubts about Ed Miliband were not overwhelming but they were sufficient enough to make me feel that we would not win in 2015. The lack of a convincing economic narrative was a problem plus some unfortunate episodes like his forgetting a large part of his conference speech in 2013, Of course, like all Labour Leaders he had some unfair press, especially when his father was used as a weapon by the Daily Mail. However, the fundamental problem was that he came across as a pleasant lecturer in politics rather than a communicator to the general public. In recent times he has returned to the Labour front bench and I think most Labour supporters would agree that he is a much more accomplished politician now than previously, when perhaps the leadership arrived a little prematurely.

Labour leaders need to study the skills of Harold Wilson, far more of an intellectual than most, but one who was able to relate his thinking to a wider audience.

Back on the doorstep, and moving to the latter half of the decade, the hostility to Jeremy Corbyn was much more pronounced. I know many in the party still passionately support Mr Corbyn, some believing that he would have become prime minister, but for some sabotaging elements in the party. I can only say as an experienced activist knocking on doors of hitherto Labour supporting households that that is questionable. Every excursion on to the stump involved being told over and over that 'you will not get our vote with Mr Corbyn as your leader.'

In 2017 I lost a County Council election by seventeen votes. A large number of voters said they were going to vote Conservative, because Mr Corbyn was my Leader. Too many of them had previously backed Labour.

Some in our party will point to the General Election of 2017 which although we lost was better than predicted. Jeremy Corbyn campaigned well against a hapless Mrs May and I especially enjoyed his handling of the Paxman interview, which he did so much more adroitly than Ed Miliband had done in 2015, when the arrogant Paxman had rubbed it in by asking Miliband on air whether he was all right. In reality, the better-than-expected performance in 2017 had much to do with the way Mrs May had framed the need for the election, one that she had said she would never call. She said she needed a stronger mandate to proceed with the leaving of the EU and the remainers, if they wished to deny her that mandate, had little alternative but to vote Labour, notwithstanding the obvious ambiguity in our position.

Mrs May then proceeded to govern as if she had secured the mandate she wanted, goaded by her irreconcilable right wing and by a press that regularly castigated the parliament that the people had elected for trying to thwart the will of the British people. The marginality of the 2017 election really demanded cross party consensus in parliament, but possibly May found that difficult with the then Labour leadership.

Now in of 2023 we have a Labour leader I did vote for.

There is a natural caution within the party because for the last hundred years when Labour has been one of the two prospective parties of Government only three leaders, Attlee, Wilson, and Blair have won outright majorities in general elections.

I have read a recent commentator recalling the view of Callaghan in 1979, that every generation sees a radical change in the public perspective, and that it is possible that we are seeing a break from neo liberal, individualistic, small state populism, to something more cohesive, communitarian and generous. Let us hope so, but we wait and see. The right wing and its media will not retire gracefully.

To win a general election, Labour will need to build a coalition of voters who want to end the period of Conservative hegemony. That means both left and right of the Labour constituency but also Liberal Democrats, Greens, moderate Conservatives tired of the rightward lurch and also that increasing constituency of people who vote for Independents in local elections. The current opinion polls suggest a Labour majority in the forthcoming election. I hope we do not assume a narrow partisan view if that is the case because such a result will be, in part, delivered by voters from wider political foundations. I hope our leadership is mindful of the aspirations of all the voters who, possibly through tactical voting, help to create the majority. Given the seriousness of the challenges to be faced, the government will need a broad coalition of support against the inevitable anti progressive strength of the British media.

We know the leadership takes a cautious path, loath to allow any hostages to fortune. There is a strong team of able politicians around Keir Starmer and the more they present as a team the better.

For, Attlee, Wilson and Blair did not lead alone. I remember Attlee's name from my childhood but Ernie Bevin, Nye Bevan and Herbert Morrison were also household names, at least in our household: in Wilson's time there were others of enormous substance such as Healey, Jenkins and Barbara Castle and Blair of course had Brown, not to mention Straw and Harriet Harman. These politicians were not always loyally dedicated to their master but they surely conveyed the impression of Labour as a party of substance.

It would be refreshing if the media could see beyond giving Keir Starmer a short soundbite, and listen too for the voices of Bridget Phillipson, Yvette Cooper, and Wes Streeting. According to the New Statesman Rachel Reeves will have the greatest influence on the next election.

Criticism of the Labour leadership does not come exclusively from the Tories. There are those on the left of our party, some very loyal to the previous leader, who are instinctively critical of Keir Starmer

There are things that he has said that I do not agree with.

However, with the emergence of National Conservatism and Trumpian sponsorship in the Tory party, this is not the time to be overly fastidious. We cannot all have our own bespoke party and bespoke leader and there is a need for personal compromises to effect the change that is so sorely needed.

We need to change the way we do politics, the way we recruit better people into politics, the way politics is reported and the way we reach key decisions, with less discussion around diametric opposites and more understanding of commonality between groups and individuals.

As it happens, in a modest setting, I had the opportunity between 2019 and 2022 to be centrally involved in a different kind of politics, leading an administration of five different groups in my own borough council. I will expand on that in my final chapter.

10

YES, LEADER

During this period of depressing politics from 2010, I continued to stand in local government elections, always with a sense of inevitable futility. I was returned in Borough Council elections in 2011, 2015 and 2019, and I also had another four years on the Kent County Council. There I was deputy leader and Labour spokesman on the economy, which I found interesting but powerless. The Kent County Council in this period was enthusiastic about what they called transformation, which simply meant cutting the costs and quality of services, by commissioning out to the private and charitable sector. As some of these services were vitally important to individuals in need of care, it was not difficult to oppose this approach.

It has profited the county council little, as persistent shortcomings in government funding have left Kent in a parlous financial position, forced to make cuts that lead to cries of anguish around the county.

The Swale borough elections of 2015, on the same day as the General Election, saw the Conservatives winning thirty two seats and Labour a mere four. I was tired enough of always being in opposition, and this level of impotence did not seem to be worth the effort.

The prospects seemed little better by 2017 and with local elections due again in 2019, I considered whether not to stand again.

It was now forty years since I was first elected to this council.

There was no prospect of Labour, acting alone, reversing this Tory hegemony. We had neither the campaigning resources nor, as I indicated in discussing our leadership at this time, did we have the necessary electoral good will. To improve on our very modest representation, we would need to target ruthlessly and concentrate on local issues in a limited number of seats.

However, I began to ponder the potential impact of other parties, such as the Liberal Democrats and Greens, who were not then on the council. Could they concentrate equally ruthlessly on a limited range of seats, where we could not seriously campaign? What would be the impact on the Conservative Party of having to fight against different opponents on different fronts?

Thus, without agreeing any electoral pact, we started discussions in which we exchanged views on our respective targeting strategies. In many cases, this led to campaigning over a period of eighteen months that helped voters identify which party in their wards offered the best challenge to the then administration.

I talked first to the Green Party, then with Liberal Democrats and finally to Councillor Mike Baldock who had backed me in Borden long ago and who was putting together an alliance of Swale Independents, principally opposed to Government planning policies. They could go where Labour feared to tread.

Our joint aim was to radically reduce the size of the overall Conservative majority and possibly push them into minority control.

The Conservatives played their part, showing an unpopular partiality for massive rural developments to meet their own government's housing allocations. They had also made a song and a dance about regenerating the town of Sittingbourne with promises that went back over a decade and with no tangible outcomes. Then just prior to the election, the Conservative leader got himself into a hole and kept on digging. Casually, he appeared on Twitter to lend support to the leader of the English Defence League. He might have been wise to immediately withdraw and apologise but he dug in, claiming to be a champion of free speech and getting himself a bit exposed on BBC Newsnight. He probably thought it would play well with some voters, but it did not with most voters.

The actual results in May 2019 were somewhat more dramatic than anticipated.

The seats won were

Conservatives 16
Labour 11
Swale Independents 10
Liberal Democrats 5
Greens 2
Other Independents 2
UKIP 1.

The Leader of the Council lost his seat to the Green Party and other prominent councillors fell. The Conservatives were still the largest party but 16 seats were too few to form any kind of administration and they indicated that they would go into opposition, if the remaining members could form a coalition.

For a range of reasons, I thought it fell to me, as Labour leader to set things in motion. We held immediate meetings of five group leaders, two of whom, Ben Martin of the Lib Dems and Tim Valentine of the Greens, had only just been elected as councillors. We did not involve the sole UKIP member, so this was a five-party coalition and within a fortnight we had agreed on a policy programme, the substantial elements of which were

- Reform of council decision making, leading to the replacement of the cabinet system with committees involving the whole council
- The provision of more affordable housing both through the planning system and through the council's own resources
- Making significant improvements to our open spaces, our coastline and our town centres and raising the profile of our local heritage
- Giving stronger support to our local economy
- Becoming a beacon of good practice at a local level in tackling the climate emergency
- And building stronger links with our local communities, health and social care and our voluntary and charitable organisations.

This was an agreed package and a radical departure from the previous administration. It contained many parts from the Swale Labour Manifesto on which we had campaigned in the election. But crucially it also reflected the general outlook of our coalition friends.

I always felt comfortable with this partnership. Every seat won by the Green Party is a rebuff to the climate deniers. The Independents are strong advocates of localism and local democracy, whilst the Liberal Democrats, after the unfortunate period of the Clegg leadership, appear to be a social liberal and social democratic party again, as they were under Ashdown and Kennedy.

They would, however, endear themselves a little more to progressive partners if they could develop a way of winning elections without the tendentious bar graphs, the questionable claims on winnability and the often dodgy boasts about their candidates being more local to the contested wards than other candidates.

Thus, at this very late point in my political life, I became Leader of Swale Council and Mike Baldock, of the Swale Independents became Deputy. I also took on the role of Portfolio Holder for Finance and Mike assumed responsibility for his favoured interest, the inevitably sensitive and contentious task of reviewing the Local Plan, against the pressures of what were excessive housing allocation demands from central government. Ben became Cabinet Member for Housing and Tim for the Environment and Climate Change, Monique Bonney, an Independent took on Economic Development and Health went to Angela Harrison of my party and Community to Richard Palmer from Mike's group. Given the collective lack of experience they did remarkably well. I asked them to lead their portfolios, establish their authority by getting on top of the detail and answer publicly for their departmental performance. They exceeded my expectations. I believe we had gathered together more collective talent than was likely to exist in most single parties in local government level.

This could be a general argument for wide ranging coalition or it could just be fortunate that all the leaders of the coalition brought an unusual degree of expertise to the table, and an ability to develop new progressive ideas.

I certainly felt that a five-group coalition was something special. Unlike the Coalition Government of 2010-2015 there was no dominant party. Labour had the most seats, but only eleven out of thirty, and so every decision had to embrace us all. Such a coalition needs leadership or it will drift. It also demands diplomacy. Local councillors can have sensitive egos.

In the event, we were never perfect and we were never free of internal tensions but we delivered a great deal, against a background of a pandemic, financial restraints and running the council for two years without a Chief Executive, as we waited sadly and forlornly for our chief Mark Radford to recover from his illness. When we finally set out to recruit a replacement, I gave up the whole of August 2020 to encouraging a range of good candidates to want to work with us.

Officers in local government have a difficult role, managing a business but continually having to defer to politicians whose instincts can be slightly different. We have been well served by ours but our election in 2019 was a culture change for them. They may have found it difficult in a multi-party administration to always divine the direction of travel and after many years of what seemed to us to be sleepy Tory rule, they may also have found the demands for constant action stressful. The financial restraints imposed by central government make priority setting an essential tool for both local politician and administrators.

We had achieved a position of authority for the Labour party in this council because we were ready to talk to and work with other groups. The alternative was to continue being irrelevant. How we did this and how we sustained the coalition are in my view a legitimate subject of interest after the local elections of 2023.

To do the best for our local community, I was prepared to be pragmatic.

We had a Conservative Government, a Conservative County Council and Conservative Members of Parliament and if engagement with political colleagues across the divide could help Swale residents, then I would do that. In particular, I worked with the Sittingbourne and Sheppey MP Gordon Henderson to determine a strategy to improve secondary schooling on the Isle of Sheppey and to secure levelling up funding from his government. The MP for Faversham showed less inclination to engage, possibly expecting me to be a kind of municipalised Jeremy Corbyn.

I will not overstate the importance of leading politically on a Borough Council. There are more demanding roles. However, it does call for leadership qualities and I embarked on this unexpected path just a little unsure.

Would I really have the required gravitas? Would I be capable of making sometimes lonely key decisions? Would I take responsibility for inevitable setbacks and could I deal with equanimity the harsh comments made by opponents and public?

I can only say that I am pleased that I was given the opportunity. It was not something I could have anticipated back in 2016 when I was anxious about my health.

Our period of office, of course, was less than a year old when the vicious Covid pandemic struck and this added exponentially to the challenges we faced.

We started well. In the week beginning March 16 2020, we held two days of meetings. With no Chief Executive our Regeneration Director Emma Wiggins took consummate control and got staff working at home and councillors ready to work remotely. We held our last council chamber meeting on March 18 and did not return for many months. We responded quickly to the demands of government, for support through community hubs and for grants to be paid out to local businesses. Our clear and instant decision making, a tribute to both politicians and local government officers, was in marked contrast to the incoherent and dithering uncertainties from the Johnson Government in that critical first stage of the crisis. Throughout the crisis we not only managed the day by day challenges but worked consistently to establish a resilient outcome once the pandemic passed its peak. The government never seemed to be able to match the effort not just of ourselves but the whole of local government at all levels.

Yet for a period late in 2020, we became the most infected borough in the country as we appeared to be cradle for a new Covid variant.

This led to an avalanche of media requests for interviews which, in the circumstances, were stressful. We were not helped by Conservative MPs in Kent, like Tugenhadt in Tonbridge and Green in Ashford, who ought to have known better, implying that their constituencies were being made to conform to health regulations because of the problems caused by Swale. I received offensive e mails from outside our area castigating us for allowing the virus to spread.

For the sake of consistency and continuity, I insisted on taking all the media interviews myself and for one week alone I spoke to the whole range of television news services, radio, the Press Association, and the *Guardian* newspaper, most of them talking to me as if we were the public health authority and the NHS rolled into one.

This was possibly because Emma and I had set up an inter-agency group that included public health, the police, our local prisons, local business, and the local voluntary sector to manage the impact of the pandemic. When the time came, we openly pressed for test and trace and then for vaccination centres. Taking high profile action perhaps led to the assumption of high-level responsibility and it was difficult to explain to one radio station over breakfast interviews that Swale council was not literally the public health authority and we did not have the answers to all questions.

Throughout the pandemic I felt we maintained control, at least of those things for which we were responsible. I met with cabinet and officers every Monday, and we systematically reviewed progress on matters such as our community hub, our support to businesses and the level of compliance with the health regulations. Every Wednesday I met with leaders across Kent and we got clear briefings from public health officers from Kent and Medway. Emma Wiggins and I spoke every Thursday. I frequently attended meetings of the District Councils Network where discussions were held, usually with junior ministers, who were generally amenable. Their problem was that they were frequently struggling to embrace the confusing direction coming from Number 10 and the Cabinet Office. I must add too, that thanks to the pressure from all district councils, the government, though carrying out a long term policy of parsimony in funding local government, often with awful consequences, were more generous than I expected in compensating councils for the costs of fighting the pandemic.

I think we did very well and I think local government in general did very well. The case for devolution of central government business to local communities is often framed in a political context, of encouraging local democracy. But the story of the pandemic offers another perhaps more persuasive argument, and that is that local government can deliver a much wider range of public services than it currently does, in a more efficient and cost effective way than a centrally geared government. The trouble is that when I have heard Conservative politicians make a case for devolution, it sounds more like setting up local government as an arm of central government, to carry out instructions based on centralised decision making. I am not sure about elected mayors everywhere either.

As I have said, I was very happy to have had this opportunity to lead, in a unique governance situation and at a unique period of pressure on local government. My willingness to engage with leaders of other Councils in Kent had its reward during the pandemic. For a time, we were under greater pressure than our colleagues, who rather than gloating over our predicament, provided genuine support, particularly when I called sternly for our residents to observe the public health restrictions that were necessary to keep us safe. These colleagues in Kent were, of course, predominantly Conservative and their attitude contrasted by some Kent Tory MPs.

And what did I achieved personally? Having spent a decade excoriating our opponents for their handling of the Sittingbourne regeneration project, we now had to make it work. We found that contracts had not been secured with tenants. Building work had commenced that was contrary to the planning permission. A multi storey car park had stopped construction because of disagreements with the development company and a key component of the project, high rise housing, was plainly unviable. It took two years to sort all this out. It is working well but as with so much in our current economic climate, we have to hope it remains viable.

I am pleased too, that we have shifted a lot of priority spending on to the neglected Isle of Sheppey, making Sheerness the target for our levelling up bid to government. I also did what I could to raise the importance of skills and education to improve our local economy.

But, my biggest challenge, was naturally to keep the coalition of parties working together. Mentally I began to see myself as a coalition rather than a Labour politician. I took pride in the work of all my colleagues and inevitably began to applaud by-election successes elsewhere in the country for their parties, if they were at the expense of the Conservatives rather than Labour. We all endeavoured to emphasize our common aims and avoided areas of ideological difference.

The durability of our administration was built on good respectful relationships, re-enforced by regular and cheerful Monday morning informal meetings. Since the first lockdown we met remotely on our laptops, in studies, kitchens and bedrooms around the borough.

One part of the role of leader that I have been mildly uneasy with is being addressed in meetings as 'Leader' rather than by name. But it is what happens now in local government, the tone being set by senior officers. I have seen instances of it going to people's heads and, of course, some 'Yes, Leader' responses probably carry as much genuine regard as a 'Yes, Prime Minister' from Sir Humphrey Appleby to a puffed-up Jim Hacker.

However, for all our good intentions and goodwill, critical points did occur. One was bizarrely over the precise siting of a much-needed public toilet for visitors to the very pleasant Minster Leas coastline on Sheppey. Our professional advice was that there could only be one site, from an engineering point of view. Local people disagreed and some members of our cabinet supported them. I am afraid I took the view that another long process of consultation would only delay the building of a key facility and that we would either end up without the investment or have it in the only plausible place. So, whilst key members of the Cabinet were reluctant to agree, I asked for collective support and we went ahead, notwithstanding we did receive a mild rebuke from the Local Government Ombudsman. The Conservative opposition got very exercised about our disregard for local views and expressed Olympian indignation when I observed that we were building a small public toilet not a nuclear power station.

The Conservative position was not so surprising as they had probably lost seats in 2019 because there was a common view that they did not listen to local views.

These days, when I go to Minster, I only hear people's appreciation of what we did and I was pleased to read in an article on good places to go to in Kent, that Minster was singled out for commendation, partly owing to the high quality of its public toilet.

We have recently had a Council by election and Labour canvassed in the area of greatest opposition. And guess what? Nobody is complaining now and one resident pleaded with us not to allow it to be closed.

The fact is we were running a Cabinet system, and despite our eclectic makeup, collective cabinet responsibility was important.

There was one area where my view was not unanimously supported. When Tony Blair introduced the Cabinet system into local government, he also provided for Scrutiny panels to hold the narrow administrations to account. During the time that I was Leader and we were running a Cabinet system, I insisted that the Opposition Tories should Chair the panel. Some of my colleagues believed the Tories had forfeited that right by retaining that Chair when they were in office and suggested I was too tolerant.

In fact, they were a harmless opposition and quite often it was members supporting the administration who asked the more searching questions. Part of the appeal of the coalition was around openness and I did not think our retaining the Chair of Scrutiny could possibly be right or defensible. Once we moved to a Committee system the question disappeared.

I have given this account of our Swale Coalition because something like our modest experience in an uncelebrated part of North Kent may someday have to be emulated in our dire Westminster climate.

Can I humbly offer some thoughts on coalition politics? First, it is not enough to be drawn together simply to keep the Conservatives or anyone else out of office. There needs to be a sense of political purpose and the Leader has a key role in this, establishing a vision in the first place, but continually articulating it to colleagues and the wider public. There has too, to be administrative competence, good business management and good communications. But there also must not be fear. It is no good simply trimming and prevaricating for fear that the alliance might collapse and, as I frequently stressed to my colleagues, if you have the numbers do not worry too much about the opposition. There is a job to do. Elections can wait. The current Conservative government has failed for many reasons, but one weakness has been a perpetual concentration on short term political opinion making. It only betrays a sense of insecurity, with the current government always manifestly too concerned about their own right wing and their distrust of each other. The current prime minister has shown himself to lack the kind of leadership that is needed if we are to tackle very serious existential issues, like the climate emergency and our domestic need for infrastructure investment.

As a country we have a choice.

Either continue with the toxic politics of name calling and aggression, of ill-founded partisanship, of myths and prejudice and the interminable wish to preserve the prevailing ideological obsessions of the neo liberal 1980s; or find a kinder, more collegiate, more informed and more genuinely patriotic path, where we negotiate our way together through the critical issues we face, where we do not always think our views are the only legitimate ones and we sincerely consider the needs and rights of everyone, not a privileged and entitled few. Our current mores and system do not lend themselves to the better latter path.

I confess that this call for a kinder more collegiate politics may fit a little ill with my comments about the Conservative party in these later chapters. But that is the point. Unless the Tories can recover their sanity, reject narrow and impractical ideology, and replace populist slogans with reasoned evidenced thinking, we cannot attain the goal of a better type of politics with them in government.

I do not relish the idea of Conservative extinction, which is not going to happen anyway, but one of my lifelong fixed ideas has always been, based on the German experience of 1932, that the collapse of conventional Conservatism can only lead to the rise of the authoritarian right, even when that authoritarianism is masked behind a bogus libertarianism.

Politics over the next few years is full of unknowns. Like many others, I would like to see a change of direction, away from the crude populism and insularity of recent years. We need a political leadership that is simply more enlightened, able genuinely to tackle our transparent problems, more internationalist in outlook, aware of the need for intervention and funding for a more equitable society.

Labour has to lead this change. It has to be deep seated, not just a variation on a failing theme. But I want to repeat what I said in the previous chapter. If Labour forms a majority government sometime next year with the obvious benefit of tactical voting by supporters of other political traditions, then I hope we can seek out what we have in common with those parties and engage with them in policy decisions. There is a majority mainstream of thinking that can reject the extreme tendency towards individualism, populism, scapegoating, cultural divisions, and intolerance. Labour can lead that mainstream change but its values are not exclusive to us. I hope a majority Labour government will reach out not only to other left of centre parties but also to the moderate and sane sections of the Conservative party.

Back in 2019 when our five Leaders agreed to a coalition partnership, I agreed to be Leader but explained I would be prepared to stand down after two years, so that others could lead into the future. In the event, things were so hectic by 2021 and we were still helping our Chief Executive to settle, so I did not raise the issue of change and neither did anyone else. However, I wanted to honour our agreement and in March of 2022 I announced my intention to pass the Leadership on to someone who, unlike me, would be standing in the 2023 elections. For the final year of the coalition, Mike Baldock took on the burdens of leadership.

During the recent elections, I acted as agent for the Labour Party, anxious to ensure that we could continue to play a major part in the council, sharing power across a range of parties. As it happened, we increased our share of seats, became the largest party for the first time in over thirty years, and my Labour friend Tim Gibson is now Leader of the Council.

So, I have ended my time as a local Councillor, and I have more time for other things, especially my wife and family.

But it is impossible to stop completely being a politician. The current state of politics and our country is too critical to just hide away. Forgive the presumption, but something like Burke's counsel that evil triumphs when good men do nothing.

We are at a crossroads that, in many ways, seems dangerous, but there is hope.

Making our politics work better is naturally a challenge

to politicians but it is also a challenge to the electorate and the media that has played its part in bringing us to where we are. Our education has not served our democracy well. Apathy and cynicism will not get us to a better place. Involvement and participation are a better form of patriotism than rejection and cultural hostility.

I believe the inside left of politics has a crucial part to play.

THE END